COMPUTERS, INTERNET, AND SOCIETY

Computers in the Workplace

COMPUTERS,
INTERNET,
AND SOCIETY

Computers in the Workplace

Robert Plotkin

Facts On File
An Infobase Learning Company

COMPUTERS IN THE WORKPLACE

Facts On File, Inc.
An imprint of Infobase Learning
132 West 31st Street
New York NY 10001

Library of Congress Cataloging-in-Publication Data

Plotkin, Robert, 1971–
   Computers in the workplace / Robert Plotkin.
     p. cm.
   Includes bibliographical references and index.
   ISBN 978-0-8160-7758-8
1. Office practice—Automation—Juvenile literature. 2. Management—Computer programs—Juvenile literature. 3. Organizational change—Juvenile literature. I. Title.
   HF5548.P56 2012
   658.2'7—dc23
                                2011015392

Facts On File books are available at special discounts when purchased in bulk quantities for businesses, associations, institutions, or sales promotions. Please call our Special Sales Department in New York at (212) 967-8800 or (800) 322-8755.

You can find Facts On File on the World Wide Web at http://www.infobaselearning.com

Text design by Kerry Casey
Composition by Hermitage Publishing Services
Illustrations by Bobbi McCutcheon
Photo research by Suzanne M. Tibor
Cover printed by Yurchak Printing, Landisville, Pa.
Book printed and bound by Yurchak Printing, Landisville, Pa.
Date printed: March 2012

Printed in the United States of America

This book is printed on acid-free paper.

CONTENTS

PREFACE

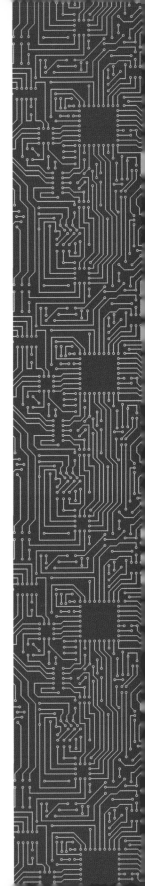

Computers permeate innumerable aspects of people's lives. For example, computers are used to communicate with friends and family, analyze finances, play games, watch movies, listen to music, purchase products and services, and learn about the world. People increasingly use computers without even knowing it, as microprocessors containing software replace mechanical and electrical components in everything from automobiles to microwave ovens to wristwatches.

Conversations about computers tend to focus on their technological features, such as how many billions of calculations they can perform per second, how much memory they contain, or how small they have become. We have good reason to be amazed at advances in computer technology over the last 50 years. According to one common formulation of Moore's law (named after Gordon Moore of Intel Corporation), the number of transistors on a chip doubles roughly every two years. As a result, a computer that can be bought for $1,000 today is as powerful as a computer that cost more than $1 million just 15 years ago.

Although such technological wonders are impressive in their own right, we care about them not because of the engineering achievements they represent but because they have changed how people interact every day. E-mail not only enables communication with existing friends and family more quickly and less expensively but also lets us forge friendships with strangers halfway across the globe. Social networking platforms such as Twitter and Facebook enable nearly instant, effortless communication among large groups of people without requiring the time or effort needed to compose and read e-mail messages. These and other forms of communication are facilitated by increasingly powerful mobile handheld devices, such as the BlackBerry and iPhone, which make it possible for people to communicate at any time and in any place, thereby eliminating the need for a desktop computer with a hardwired Internet connection. Such improvements in technology have led to changes in society, often in complex and unexpected ways.

Understanding the full impact that computers have on society therefore requires an appreciation of not only what computers can do but also how computer technology is used in practice and its effects on human behavior and attitudes.

Computers, Internet, and Society is a timely multivolume set that seeks to provide students with such an understanding. The set includes the following six titles, each of which focuses on a particular context in which computers have a significant social impact:

- *Communication and Cyberspace*
- *Computer Ethics*
- *Computers and Creativity*
- *Computers in Science and Mathematics*
- *Computers in the Workplace*
- *Privacy, Security, and Cyberspace*

It is the goal of each volume to accomplish the following:

- explain the history of the relevant computer technology, what such technology can do today, and how it works;
- explain how computers interact with human behavior in a particular social context; and
- encourage readers to develop socially responsible attitudes and behaviors in their roles as computer users and future developers of computer technology.

New technology can be so engrossing that people often adopt it—and adapt their behavior to it—quickly and without much forethought. Yesterday's students gathered in the schoolyard to plan for a weekend party; today they meet online on a social networking Web site. People flock to such new features as soon as they come available, as evidenced by the long lines at the store every time a newer, smarter phone is announced.

Most such developments are positive. Yet they also carry implications for our privacy, freedom of speech, and security, all of which are easily overlooked if one does not pause to think about them. The paradox of today's computer technology is that it is both everywhere and invisible. The goal of this set is to make such technology visible so that it, and its impact on society, can be examined, as well as to assist students in using conceptual tools for making informed and responsible decisions about how to both apply and further develop that technology now and as adults.

Although today's students are more computer savvy than all of the generations that preceded them, many students are more familiar with what computers can do than with how computers work or the social changes being wrought by computers. Students who use the Internet constantly may remain unaware of how computers can be used to invade their privacy or steal their identity or how journalists and human rights activists use computer encryption technology to keep their communications secret and secure from oppressive governments around the world. Students who have grown up copying information from the World Wide Web and downloading songs, videos, and feature-length films onto computers, iPods, and cell phones may not understand the circumstances under which those activities are legitimate and when they violate copyright law. And students who have only learned about scientists and inventors in history books probably are unaware that today's innovators are using computers to discover new drugs and write pop music at the touch of a button.

In fact, young people have had such close and ongoing interactions with computers since they were born that they often lack the historical perspective to understand just how much computers have made their lives different from those of their parents. Computers form as much of the background of students' lives as the air they breathe; as a result, they tend to take both for granted. This set, therefore, is highly relevant and important to students because it enables them to understand not only how computers work but also how computer technology has affected their lives. The goal of this set is to provide students with the intellectual tools needed to think critically about computer technology so that they can make informed and responsible decisions about how to both use and further develop that technology now and as adults.

This set reflects my long-standing personal and professional interest in the intersection between computer technology, law, and society. I started programming computers when I was about 10 years old and my fascination with the technology has endured ever since. I had the honor of studying computer science and engineering at the Massachusetts Institute of Technology (MIT) and then studying law at the Boston University School of Law, where I now teach a course entitled, "Software and the Law." Although I spend most of my time as a practicing patent lawyer, focusing on patent protection for computer technology, I have also spoken and written internationally on topics including patent protection for software, freedom of speech, electronic privacy, and ethical implications of releasing potentially harmful software. My book, *The Genie in the Machine,* explores the impact of computer-automated inventing on law, businesses, inventors, and consumers.

What has been most interesting to me has been to study not any one aspect of computer technology, but rather to delve into the wide range of ways in which such technology affects, and is affected by, society. As a result, a multidisciplinary set such as this is a perfect fit for my background and interests. Although it can be challenging to educate non-technologists about how computers work, I have written and spoken about such topics to audiences including practicing lawyers, law professors, computer scientists and engineers, ethicists, philosophers, and historians. Even the work that I have targeted solely to lawyers has been multidisciplinary in nature, drawing on the history and philosophy of computer technology to provide context and inform my legal analysis. I specifically designed my course on "Software and the Law" to be understandable to law students with no background in computer technology. I have leveraged this experience in explaining complex technical concepts to lay audiences in the writing of this multidisciplinary set for a student audience in a manner that is understandable and engaging to students of any background.

The world of computers changes so rapidly that it can be difficult even for those of us who spend most of our waking hours learning about the latest developments in computer technology to stay up to date. The term *technological singularity* has even been coined to refer to a point, perhaps not too far in the future, when the rate of technological change will become so rapid that essentially no time elapses between one technological advance and the next. For better or worse, time does elapse between writing a series of books such as this and the date of publication. With full awareness of the need to provide students with current and relevant information, every effort has been made, up to the time at which these volumes are shipped to the printers, to ensure that each title in this set is as up to date as possible.

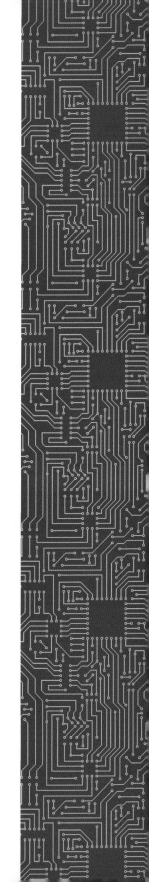

ACKNOWLEDGMENTS

Many people deserve thanks for making this series a reality. First, my thanks to my literary agent, Jodie Rhodes, for introducing me to Facts On File. When she first approached me, it was to ask whether I knew any authors who were interested in writing a series of books on a topic that I know nothing about—I believe it was biology. In response, I asked whether there might be interest in a topic closer to my heart—computers and society—and, as they say, the rest is history.

Frank Darmstadt, my editor, has not only hand my held through all of the high-level planning and low-level details involved in writing a series of this magnitude, but also he exhibited near superhuman patience in the face of drafts whose separation in time could be marked by the passing of the seasons. He also helped me to toe the fine dividing line between the forest and the trees, and between today's technological marvels and tomorrow's long-forgotten fads—a distinction that is particularly difficult to draw prospectively in the face of rapidly changing technology. I also appreciate the incisive reviews and copyediting from Michael Axon and Alexandra Simon.

Several research assistants, including Catie Watson, Rebekah Judson, Jessica McElrath, Sue Keeler, Samuel Smith, and Kristen Lighter, provided invaluable aid in uncovering and summarizing information about technologies ranging from the ancient to the latest gadgets we carry in our pockets. In particular, Luba Jabsky performed extensive research that formed the foundation of many of the book's chapters and biographies.

As the saying goes, a picture is worth a thousand words, and this set comes to life through the artwork and photographs it contains. Although computer science, with its microscopic electronic components and abstract software modules, is a particularly difficult field to illustrate visually, artist Bobbi McCutcheon and photo researcher Suzie Tibor could not have matched visuals to text more perfectly.

Last, but not least, I thank my family, including my partner, Melissa, and my dog, Maggie, for standing by my side and at my feet, respectively, as I spent my evenings and weekends trying, through words and pictures, to convey some of the wonder and excitement in computer technology that I felt as a teenager to the next generation.

INTRODUCTION

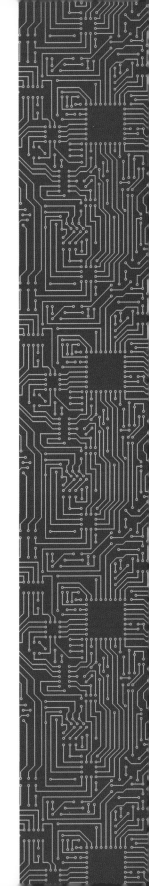

Both employees and employers in a wide variety of fields have benefited from computers and the Internet. According to a 2009 study by the Internet Advertising Bureau, the Internet contributes about $300 billion to the GDP (gross domestic product) of the United States and has created 1.2 million jobs. At the same time, the rapid and radical nature of the advances in digital technology over the last 50 years has created significant challenges in the workplace, as both workers and business owners have needed to adapt to such technology or face losing to the competition. *Computers in the Workplace* discusses how digital technology has affected businesses, addressing topics such as the systemization of work, the division of labor, outsourcing, and crowdsourcing.

In agrarian America, most individuals were sole proprietors of their own trade or craft. As the Industrial Revolution began and the *assembly line* and the factory were created, the way people worked fundamentally changed. For example, instead of a small town being composed of a blacksmith, a farmer, and a doctor, many entire towns migrated to nearby urban centers. The benefits of such a move were clear: assembly line jobs paid more, schools were better, and there was more entertainment. As a result, though, the newly emerging middle class was trained to work on assembly lines, and the assembly line requires a factory, which requires a boss and management. People were no longer the sole proprietors of their own businesses.

Though many corporations still thrive, the assembly line has all but left the United States. The result has been what anyone would expect: a working class spread haphazardly across the continent with few local jobs to match their skills. To meet the demands of this type of workforce, new services and business models have emerged that create opportunity for people of all different professions to prosper in an interconnected, digital world.

Chapter 1 explains the technological and cultural changes leading up to the invention of the computer. The assembly line, developed and popularized in the early 1900s by Ford Motor Company, contributed to the rise of the middle class by paying high wages and creating affordable goods, turning a company's workers into its customers. Assembly line production was more efficient than traditional holistic methods because workers only needed to be trained for a single skill that would be honed with experience and repetition.

Chapter 2 discusses the history and current state of machines in manufacturing. Manufacturing robots are known for their efficiency, accuracy, and speed and are a popular choice for production lines, particularly in the automobile industry. Automatic process control systems can detect dangerous conditions, such as high temperatures in the core of a nuclear power plant, and sound alarms in response. Modern technologies, such as desktop fabrication, allow designers to upload digital blueprints of products to be created entirely by a manufacturing machine.

Chapter 3 discusses how the invention of computers has affected administrative assistants, secretaries, and other clerical workers. Early typewriters required a forceful stroke to push the mechanical arm down onto the paper. This was arduous and severely limited typing speeds. Dictation was usually taken by hand to be typed later. To make copies, secretaries manually retyped multiple copies of the same document. Today, word processors, speech recognition software, high-speed printers and photocopiers, and a variety of other computer technologies have enabled secretaries to transform themselves from clerical workers to office managers, taking responsibility for doing everything from organizing conferences to designing brochures, while leaving the low-level details to computers and the Internet.

Chapter 4 addresses several industries that are able to complete a great deal of their work with industry-standard software packages. Accountants, instead of keeping books by hand, use accounting software to create budgets, make budget forecasts, compare budgets to expenses, and generate detailed accounting reports. Project management software can be used to allocate people and resources efficiently across large organizations. Sales staff can use customer relationship management software to keep track of orders. Advertising and marketing teams can reach an audience several orders of magnitude larger with the use of Internet advertising.

Chapter 5 shows how computer programmers use computers to create software. Computers can only understand ones and zeroes. Even the earliest programmers realized this was unfeasible and developed low-level machine languages, such as assembly languages, to more easily manipulate bits and bytes on the hard disk or memory. Today's high-level programming languages are far more powerful than assembly language, but computers still only read data in ones and zeroes. Programmers use compilers to transform programs written in high-level programming languages into assembly language and then into bits and bytes. As a result, programmers are able to create software using highly abstract instructions, without needing to understand how the hardware of the computer executes such instructions.

Chapter 6 addresses how the legal profession uses technology to simplify tasks such as online legal research, document assembly, tracking deadlines, and electronic court filing. Before computers, many lawyers had to maintain their own legal libraries at their offices. These encyclopedic reference texts were expensive, time-consuming to sift through, and could fill an entire room. The development of online legal search engines such as LexisNexis makes legal research simpler, faster, less expensive, and more reliable.

Chapter 7 discusses how doctors use technology to treat patients. Electronic medical records save paperwork and can be beamed across the country to another doctor in minutes. Surgeons routinely use simulation software to train before operating on real patients. MRIs and CAT scans are minimally invasive procedures that allow doctors to look deep inside our bodies.

Chapter 8 is an in-depth examination of how people work in the modern age. New types of employment, such as e-lancing, outsourcing, crowdsourcing, and virtual offices promise to revolutionize the way that people work and hire. Chapter 8 also discusses the new skills that employees and entrepreneurs need to succeed in the digital age. Careers today require different skills than they did in previous generations. In fact, many of the skills taught in colleges today will likely be obsolete before these students retire. The most important skill that can be taught is how to acquire new skills for new technologies. Many artists, engineers, writers, and small business owners are using computers and the Internet to market their services, perform their accounting, and even to provide services directly to their customers. As a result, digital technology is making it easier than ever for people to become their own bosses.

As detailed in *Computers and the Workplace,* the invention and subsequent rise of the Internet has provided individuals with the ability to work in both California and New York without ever leaving a home office. Computer technology is reducing costs and providing greater flexibility for both employers and workers. At the same time, computer technology is resulting in increased competition for employers and can result in decreased demand and job security for workers. All of these changes have made businesses more profitable and more efficient but have necessitated a change in the structure, goals, and methods of business owners, managers, and frontline workers.

1

SCIENTIFIC MANAGEMENT: THE SYSTEMATIZATION OF WORK

Computer scientists are fond of saying that computers are dumb because they can only do exactly what they have been programmed by a human to do. Although such statements are made somewhat tongue in cheek, they reflect a significant feature of computers: Before a computer can perform any task, that task must first be defined in terms of a sequence of clearly specified steps by a human programmer. The task, in other words, must first be systematized before it can be automated. Although systematization must always precede automation, systematization need not always be followed by automation. Instead, systematizing a task can have significant benefits even if the systematized task is performed manually by people, rather than automatically by a computer or other machine. This chapter explores some of the many ways in which managers, business owners, and workers themselves have striven to systematize work to increase its efficiency, reliability, and effectiveness.

DIVISION OF LABOR

Factories and assembly lines are commonplace in today's industrial world. Consumers expect to see products manufactured in stages, passing from one station to another as workers—or perhaps computerized robots—add another part, tighten a bolt, or apply a layer of paint.

Long ago, workers operated differently. A single shipbuilder, for instance, might build an entire ship by himself or with a small crew, all of whom knew how all of the components of the ship were constructed and interacted with each other. Such a team would finish one ship before starting another. *Division of labor,* the process in which each worker specializes

1

in learning and performing only a single task repeatedly and in which each such task performed by each worker combines with the other tasks performed by other workers into a completed whole, was described in the late 1600s by Sir William Petty (1623–87), an English economist. Petty observed the division of labor in Dutch shipyards. The innovative Dutch used several teams, each of which specialized in performing a distinct task. Each team performed its sole task again and again for each successive ship.

Another long-ago example of the efficient use of division of labor is the Terra-cotta army commissioned by Chinese emperor Qin Shi Huangdi (259 B.C.E.–210 B.C.E.). This collection of about 8,000 life-sized clay soldiers and horses was buried with the emperor. The figures' separate body parts were manufactured by different workshops and later assembled to completion. Notably, each workshop inscribed its name on the part it manufactured to add traceability for quality control.

In the same manner, the Venetian Arsenal, at the peak of its efficiency in the early 16th century, employed some 16,000 workers who apparently were able to produce nearly a ship a day. They could fit out, arm, and provision a newly built galley with standardized parts on an assembly line basis that would not be seen again until the Industrial Revolution.

The division of labor is widely accepted and practiced in modern economies because it can produce great efficiencies, particularly for projects so complex that no single person can perform all tasks necessary to complete the project. Those who study the division of labor, however, have found advantages and problems with the system. The primary benefit is efficiency. Developing and practicing a single skill results in a worker who uses that skill more efficiently and effectively. Performing the same kind of task repeatedly also reduces the *switching costs* involved in stopping one task and starting another that can be a drag on efficiency. This is why families typically shop for groceries just once or twice a week rather than stopping by the market before every meal.

One criticism of division of labor is that it isolates workers, alienating them from the completed job. People who perform a single task may not see the fruits of their labor and come to feel like a small cog in a large machine. Another negative is that reducing complex tasks to simple ones performed separately can result in overlooking solutions to problems that can only be identified by seeing the big picture.

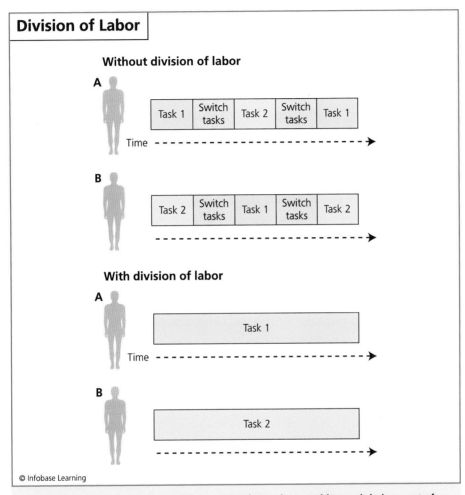

Division of Labor

Without division of labor

A

| Task 1 | Switch tasks | Task 2 | Switch tasks | Task 1 |

Time → → →

B

| Task 2 | Switch tasks | Task 1 | Switch tasks | Task 2 |

With division of labor

A

| Task 1 |

Time → → →

B

| Task 2 |

© Infobase Learning

If two tasks need to be performed by two people—such as washing and drying a set of dishes—in many circumstances those tasks can be performed more efficiently if they are split, with each performing only one task. Such assignment of separate tasks to separate people is known as division of labor. One reason that division of labor can increase efficiency is that it takes time for a person to switch from one task to another. Therefore, if each person solely performs one task continuously, dead time (shown in the figure as switch tasks) is eliminated and can instead be used to perform the task at hand.

The economist Adam Smith (1723–90) focused on how economic growth occurs. In 1776, Smith wrote in *An Inquiry into the Nature and Causes of the Wealth of Nations* (usually abbreviated as *The Wealth of Nations*) that economic growth results from increasing division of labor. Using the famous example of the manufacture of pins, he estimated that 10 workers could produce 48,000 pins per day if the process was broken down into 18 specialized tasks—such as forming the wire, straightening the wire, cutting the wire, making a point, forming the head of the pin, and polishing—assigned to particular workers. With the division of labor, individual productivity would average 4,800 pins per day. Without it, a worker would be lucky to produce even one pin per day.

This kind of growth is exactly what allowed the Industrial Revolution to flourish in the 18th and 19th centuries. Factories mushroomed as assembly line technology made manufacturing faster and cheaper. But Smith also recognized potential problems with the division of labor. He pointed out that forcing individuals to perform mundane and repetitive tasks would lead to an ignorant, dissatisfied workforce. To prevent that, he urged governments to educate workers.

Technology has played a major role as the division of labor has evolved. Between 1700 and 1900, an astounding number of technological inventions changed the world. Consider this partial list: the steam engine, the first significant source of power besides wind and water; an automatic knitting machine; a mechanical seed sower; a threshing machine; the spinning jenny, which helped automate weaving; gas lighting; the cotton gin; the steam locomotive and the first regular commercial rail service; photographs; telegraphs; dynamite; X-rays; the first automobile with an internal combustion engine; and the typewriter.

Leaping a century or two into the future, computers are having a similarly revolutionary effect on today's world economy. In *The New Division of Labor: How Computers Are Creating the Next Job Market,* economists Richard Murnane and Frank Levy examine how computers are reshaping the job market and the human skills rewarded in the marketplace. Although they acknowledge that computers have replaced many jobs once performed by people, they note two kinds of critical skills that still require the human brain. One skill is expert thinking and the ability to solve new problems that cannot be solved by rules. (If the problem could be solved by rules, a computer could do it.) Examples of this kind of thinking include a scientist's research or a chef's creation of a new dish. The second skill is complex communication, the ability to convey a particular interpretation of information to others. This skill is required for jobs such as teaching or sales. A student could get a calculus lesson from a Web site, but there is no guarantee that the student will understand the information. It takes a good teacher to present the information in a way that allows the student to comprehend and apply it.

TAYLORISM

An enduring force in modern manufacturing is *Taylorism,* named for the American industrial engineer Frederick Winslow Taylor (1856–1915) who, in his 1911 book *Principles of Scientific Management,* laid down fundamental principles for assembly line factories. Taylor became interested in improving worker productivity early in his career when he observed gross inefficiencies during his contact with steelworkers. His new methods emphasized gaining maximum efficiency and output from both machine and worker.

Before *scientific management,* work was performed by skilled craftsmen who learned their jobs in lengthy apprenticeships. Taylor's methodology subdivided every task into small and simple segments that could be analyzed and taught easily. He aimed to minimize skill requirements and therefore to reduce training time and to replace rule-of-thumb productivity estimates with precise measurements. He is also well known for the *time and motion studies* in which he tracked workers' tasks with a stopwatch, measuring specialized sets of motions to find the one best way. Taylor argued that even the most basic, mindless tasks could be planned in a way that would dramatically increase productivity.

Those old-fashioned skilled workers made their own decisions about how their jobs were to be performed. Scientific management took away much of this autonomy and converted skilled crafts into a series of simplified jobs that could be performed by unskilled workers who could be easily trained. Although justifiably criticized for alienating workers by treating them like mindless machines, Taylorism was a critical factor in the unprecedented scale of U.S. factory output that led to an Allied victory in World War II.

After years of experiments to determine optimal work methods, Taylor proposed the following four principles of scientific management:

1. Replace rule-of-thumb estimates with methods based on a scientific study of the tasks.
2. Scientifically select, train, and develop each worker.
3. Cooperate with workers to ensure that the scientifically developed methods are followed.

4. Divide work nearly equally between managers and workers, so that managers apply scientific management principles to planning the work and the workers perform the tasks.

Separating the planning of work (done by managers) from the performance of work (done by laborers) was an important aspect of Taylorism. Taylor's single-minded focus on the importance of matching the worker to the job was coupled with a prejudice against manual laborers that most people today would find repugnant, as evidenced by the following statement by Taylor: "Now one of the very first requirements for a man who is fit to handle pig iron as a regular occupation is that he shall be so stupid and so phlegmatic that he more nearly resembles in his mental make-up the ox than any other type. The man who is mentally alert and intelligent is for this very reason entirely unsuited to what would, for him, be the grinding monotony of work of this character. Therefore the workman who is best suited to handling pig iron is unable to understand the real science of doing this class of work."

Taylor's techniques were attractive to many factory owners because of their potential to increase efficiency. As a result, Taylor's principles were implemented in many factories. Henry Ford applied Taylor's principles in his automobile factories, and families even began to perform their household tasks based on the results of time and motion studies.

Ford's adaptation of Taylor's scientific management principles came to be known as *Fordism*. The automaker's manufacturing philosophy aimed to increase productivity by standardizing output, using conveyor-belt assembly lines, and dividing the work into small, simple tasks. Whereas Taylorism sought machine and worker efficiency, Fordism sought to combine machines and workers into a single unit. Fordism also emphasized minimization of costs rather than maximization of profits.

Taylorism had no major impact on the Japanese car industry until the late 1940s, after World War II. When Taylorism was introduced into Japan, Japanese traditions put a spin on the process. Rather than straightforward work study, employers relied upon group discussion and collective problem solving. Modern observers note that no company practices Taylorism better than Toyota does. The twist is that the company views employees not just as pairs of hands but as knowledge workers who accumulate experience on the company's front lines. Toyota invests heavily in people and organizational capabilities, and it garners ideas from everyone and everywhere: shop floor, office, and field. Toyota's culture places humans, not machines, at the center of the company.

THE ASSEMBLY LINE

Before the 20th century, most manufactured products were made individually by hand. A single craftsman or team of craftsmen would create each part of a product. In this process of *craft production,* workers used their skills and tools

A 1932 Ford Model A automobile on an assembly line at the Rouge Plant in Dearborn, Michigan, in 1932. Henry Ford's assembly lines, in which each worker performed only a small part of the overall manufacturing process, reflected Ford's focus on implementing a sharp division of labor in his factories. Because each assembly line worker performed the same small set of actions on the assembly line repeatedly throughout the day, relatively unskilled workers could be trained and put to work on the assembly line quickly, even if they otherwise had no skill or knowledge of mechanics or of the overall operation of the automobile. *(AP Images)*

to create individual parts, then assemble them into the final product. They made trial-and-error changes in the parts until they fit and could work together.

Mass production changed all that, using the principles of division of labor to roll out large quantities of standardized products, especially on *assembly lines*. The first assembly line for mass production was developed at the Ford Motor Company between 1908 and 1915 and would transform manufacturing around the world. Henry Ford was the first to master the assembly line, introducing practices such as standardizing production numbers and parts. Ford was also the first company to build large factories around the assembly line concept.

Assembly lines are designed for sequential organization of workers, tools or machines, and parts. The motion of workers is minimized to the greatest extent possible. All parts or assemblies are handled either by conveyors or motorized vehicles such as forklifts, with no manual lifting or moving. Each worker typically performs one simple operation.

In his autobiography, Henry Ford mentions several benefits of the assembly line, including:

- Workers do no heavy lifting
- No stooping or bending over
- No special training required
- Jobs for almost anyone
- Employment opportunities for immigrants

The gains in productivity made possible by the assembly line allowed Ford to increase worker pay from $2.50 to $5.00 per day and to reduce the hourly work-week while continually lowering the price of Ford's flagship Model T automobile. Perhaps Ford's motives were partially altruistic, but he was also trying to increase production and reduce high employee turnover.

Sociologists have explored the boredom and alienation that many assembly line workers felt, repeating the same specialized task all day long. Because factory workers often had to stand in the same place for hours and repeat the same motion hundreds of times per day, repetitive stress injuries became a major risk to occupational safety. Industrial noise in factories also proved dangerous. Even when it was not too high, workers were often prohibited from talking, because socializing detracted from work time.

00110101001010011101011010101010101011001010000

Scientific Management in the Military

In 1899, President William McKinley (1843–1901) tasked Elihu Root (1845–1937), his secretary of war, with bringing modern business practices to the U.S. armed forces. Root was a lawyer specializing in corporate affairs, and he wanted the army to run like a large modern corporation. He believed Taylor's theories could make the military better and more efficient.

The military bureaucracy embraced the centralized command and specialized operations that scientific management espoused. It subsidized development of machine tools as labor control devices. It also pioneered operations research and encouraged improvements in computerized management tools. Military techniques also filtered back into business and the rest of the government.

Today's armies still employ scientific management, with standard methods for performing each job, selected workers with appropriate abilities for each job, training for standard tasks, careful planning of work, and the elimination of interruptions.

00110101001010011101011010101010101011001010000

CRITICISMS OF SCIENTIFIC MANAGEMENT

The primary criticisms of scientific management are that it eliminates creativity from jobs, treats workers like machines, and can lead to low employee morale and high turnover rates, which actually reduce efficiency because of the need to retrain people. The practices can impede innovation because workers are not encouraged to suggest improvements in products and processes to management. Repetitive factory work can harm worker health and create unsafe work environments when speed is valued above all else.

Furthermore, some researchers suggest that performing the same task the same way every time may not be the most efficient or effective practice; changing circumstances may call for changes in techniques. Management may make decisions about how techniques are to be performed without the necessary background knowledge. Often the workers who directly perform a task as part of their jobs every day are in a better position to learn how to modify the task to enable it to be performed more efficiently, effectively, and safely than managers who are far removed from the day-to-day operations of the business.

While in many cases the new ways of working were accepted by workers, in some cases they were not. The use of stopwatches on the factory floor was a particularly strong source of conflict. Complaints that the system was dehumanizing led to a 1911 investigation by the U.S. Congress after workers at the Watertown Arsenal in Massachusetts went on strike. Eventually, investigators concluded there was no evidence that scientific management abused workers.

Applications of scientific management sometimes fail to account for two problems with the theory:

- It ignores individual differences: The most efficient way of working for one person may be inefficient for another.
- It ignores the different economic interests of workers and management, so that both the measurement processes and the retraining required by Taylor's methods would frequently be resented and sometimes sabotaged by the workforce.

Taylor acknowledged both issues, but they are often overlooked by managers who saw only potential improvements to efficiency. Taylor believed that scientific management could not work unless the worker benefitted from it. In his view, management should arrange the work in such a way that one is able to produce more and get paid more. Despite controversy, however, scientific management changed the way that work was done, and forms of it continue to be used today.

Toyota is often imitated by other companies who see its Toyota Production System as a more refined version of earlier efficiency efforts, building upon the work of Taylor and learning from his mistakes. The Japanese automaker was able to greatly reduce lead time and costs while improving quality, making it one of the world's leading manufacturers. The system focuses on two key areas: continuous improvement and respect for people. Toyota has achieved automation with a human touch, increasing efficiency, decreasing waste, and using empirical methods to set priorities and solve problems.

COMPUTERS AND SCIENTIFIC MANAGEMENT TODAY

A 1958 paper on the application of computers to business systems describes just three areas: large-volume clerical operations, unified data processing activities,

100111010010101010100110010111011010100101001

Frederick Winslow Taylor, Founder of Scientific Management

Frederick Winslow Taylor was born into a wealthy Philadelphia Quaker family in 1856. His father, Franklin Taylor, was a successful attorney; his mother, Emily Annette, an abolitionist. Taylor was homeschooled by his mother and spent several years studying and traveling around Europe before enrolling in the prestigious Phillips Exeter Academy in New Hampshire in 1872. Upon graduation, Taylor was accepted at Harvard. However, as his eyesight began to fail, he was forced to abandon his plans of attending the university. Instead, he became an apprentice patternmaker and machinist at the Enterprise Hydraulic Works in Philadelphia. In 1878, after three years as an apprentice, Taylor went to work at the Midvale Steel Company, starting as a machine shop laborer. Over the next 12 years, he rose through the ranks to become shop clerk, machinist, gang

Frederick Winslow Taylor, founder of the field of scientific management. Taylor sought to reduce the job of every worker to a set of repetitive tasks that could be dictated by management and performed by workers as efficiently as possible. (©*Jacques Boyer/Roger-Viollet/The Image Works*)

boss, foreman, head of the drawing office, and, finally, the company's chief engineer in 1884. Also during that time, Taylor enrolled in night classes and obtained a degree from Stevens Institute of Technology, graduating in 1883.

Early in his career, Taylor noticed that the steelworkers habitually operated below their capacity. He attributed this behavior to a combination of factors, including fear of job security, lack of motivation, and lack of skills and knowledge to improve productivity. Traditionally, steelwork and other kinds of skilled labor were

(continues)

100111010010101010100110010111011010100101001

(continued)

performed by craftsmen, who spent years as apprentices to acquire the necessary skills and knowledge. They had complete autonomy over their work process and ability to decide how their jobs were to be performed. Taylor concluded that workers were unmotivated to be optimally productive because they feared that high levels of production would decrease the demand for workers and thus leave many of them unemployed. Because they had a great deal of control over the production process, workers were able to convince their employer that the pace at which they worked was in fact a good pace. There was no motivation to work faster because workers were not paid by the quantity produced. Therefore, they avoided working faster because they didn't want the high levels of production to become the standard. Taylor believed that the work process could be optimized to increase efficiency instead of relying on each worker's individual expertise in creating the product.

To determine the optimal level of performance, Taylor conducted time studies, which were timed observations of a worker's production process, oriented at arriving at the most efficient way to perform a particular task. Through such studies, Taylor was able to determine things such as the optimal work and rest schedule of a worker, the best weight to be lifted by a shovel, and the most productive sequence of motions to lay bricks. As a result of applications of his findings, Taylor was able to improve workers' efficiency at the factory where he worked. Taylor also concluded that some workers were better suited than others for performance of a particular task by virtue of being stronger or more limber. Those workers best suited for a specific function should be designated for that function, while others not as well equipped for the task should be assigned elsewhere to improve the overall productivity of the company.

As a result of his studies, Taylor developed a theory known as scientific management. The theory relied on scientific research that produced most efficient and scientific solutions to management problems. Today, computers are practically inseparable from most workplace tasks, and the principles of scientific management have been adapted to incorporate the advances of technology.

Although computers offer a level of precision and organization that streamlines business practices and automates some tedious and repetitive tasks, not all solutions to performance of an individual task, selection, and training of workers who were to perform the task, and method of cooperation and division of labor between management and workers, insuring the workers' tasks are properly planned out and accurately performed.

In 1889, Taylor began a comprehensive scientific management reorganization of the manufacturing plant, which was later implemented at the Bethlehem Steel Company, Midvale Steel Company, and Cramp's Shipbuilding Company, among others. Taylor's plan outlined the duties of every worker, from the president of the company all the way down to the water boy. The application of Taylor's principles resulted in greatly improved productivity at the factories, sometimes by a factor of three or more. Scientific management has had a lasting impact not only on the work of skilled factory laborers, but also on general business practices in other fields.

Although Taylor retired at 45, he continued to promote his theory through speaking engagements. The first edition of the *Principles of Scientific Management* was published privately by the American Society of Mechanical Engineers in 1911. It was subsequently reprinted and enjoyed a wide domestic as well as international distribution. Taylor received a gold medal from the Paris Exposition of 1900 for his invention of the Taylor-White process of treating modern high-speed tools and was also awarded the Elliott Cresson gold medal by the Franklin Institute in Philadelphia. He received about 100 patents for his other inventions, was president of the American Society of Mechanical Engineers in 1905 and 1906, and authored other books and articles in technical journals.

In addition to his science career, Taylor was an amateur sportsman and won the doubles title at the U.S. Tennis Championship in Newport, Rhode Island, in 1881. In 1883, he married Louise M. Spooner. Taylor passed away in 1915 from pneumonia, survived by his widow and three adopted children.

those developments have been seen as positive. Many economists, technologists, and business consultants predicted that computers would liberate the workforce, bringing self-managed work teams and decentralized decision making. But in his book *The New Ruthless Economy,* Simon Head argues that the opposite has happened. Middle- and lower-level employees have seen their work simplified, subjected to elaborate rules, and monitored digitally to make sure that the rules are obeyed. These practices might seem familiar to Frederick Taylor if he were to visit a modern workplace.

Head notes that these changes have occurred even in highly skilled professions, such as medicine, where decision-making software in the hands of insurance companies dictates the length of patients' hospital stays and determines the treatments they will or will not receive. In lower-skill jobs, such as in the call center industry, workers follow scripting software that lays out the exact conversation, line by line, that agents must follow when speaking with customers. He argues that these computer systems devalue a worker's experience and skills and subject employees to an excessive degree of supervision.

CONCLUSIONS

Everyone agrees that it is desirable to improve the efficiency of workers so that the business that employs them can become more efficient and profitable. Scientific management has gained a worldwide following in the century since its introduction because of its ability to produce such increased efficiencies and profits in a wide variety of circumstances. The modern focus on personal productivity, with many employees themselves reading books and attending seminars on how to squeeze every last ounce of efficiency out of every task they perform in both their professional and personal lives, can trace its heritage back to scientific management and to the forces driving the Industrial Revolution itself.

Controversy continues, however, not only over whether scientific management is fair to workers, but also over whether it even achieves its own stated goals in all situations. Performing the same physical task repeatedly, especially if it involves fine motor control of the hands or remaining in one position for long periods of time, can lead to injuries that may not only remove individual employees from the workforce for extended periods of time but also increase the health care costs borne by the employer. Jobs involving direct service to customers, such as positions in sales, marketing, training, and customer service, can require the use of judgment and interpersonal skills that cannot be reduced to a fixed set of tasks repeated without variation. Finally, if the adage that variety is the spice of life is correct, then employees who are prohibited from deviating from the course fixed for them by their employers will be unfulfilled and lack motivation, leading them to seek employment elsewhere, and requiring the employer to hire and train new workers. Although it might seem paradoxical at first, the best way to maximize worker efficiency might be to allow workers themselves to inject a healthy smattering of inefficient variety into their workdays.

2

MANUFACTURING: FROM LINE WORKERS TO ROBOTS

The previous chapter explained how scientific management has been used to systematize the tasks performed by workers in an effort to maximize the efficiency of work. Once a task has been systematized by reorganizing it into a sequence of fixed steps and documenting the steps using instructions that can be carried out by a worker with little or no training, it is but a small step to design a machine to perform the same sequence of steps automatically. This chapter explores the history of robots and explains how they are being used today in a variety of industries.

ROBOTS

The earliest use of mechanical means to accomplish routine tasks can be traced to ancient history: Ctesibius of Alexandria (285–222 B.C.E.), a Greek inventor, invented a water-powered clock with gears and an hour hand in 250 B.C.E. In the late 1800s, Nicola Tesla (1856–1943), the inventor of alternating current (AC) electricity and radio, developed remotely controlled vehicles. In the 1950s and '60s, when the pace of computing and mechanical research started to accelerate, the study of *robotics* became more practical. After numerous attempts at creating *robots* with television cameras, wheels, and sensing devices, Joe Engelberger (1925–   ), known as the father of robotics, founded the Unimatics Company, which produced the *Unimate,* a robotic arm that was first used for auto assembly by General Motors in 1962. The arm, composed of jointed sections that were computer-controlled to perform a number of machining tasks, was the first universally accepted piece of robotic hardware in the workplace.

Today, most robots are still found in factories. These robots are known as *industrial robots*. Although many specialized types exist, jointed-arm robots remain the most common type. Robots—except in the movies—rarely resemble their human creators. Instead, each robot is developed to perform a certain task, with a shape that conforms to that task. Robots frequently are used in tightly controlled environments, such as on assembly lines. Materials handling (moving items around factories) is the largest application for robots, followed by spot welding. Robots also stack products on pallets for shipping, perform automated paint spraying, and test wear and resistance on consumer items.

Although the automotive industry is still the largest user of robots, robots are playing an increasingly significant role in lighter industry, such as consumer electronics and food packaging. In the cookie industry, for instance, snacks are baked, cooled, and moved on three- to four-foot-wide conveyor belts at a rate of 1,000 to 2,000 cookies a minute. For sandwich-type cookies, such as Oreos, half the belt has tops and half the belt has bottoms. A robot tracks the moving conveyor belt, picking up the tops and placing them onto the bottoms as the cookies move past. Robots farther down the line pick up the assembled cookies and stack them in trays. Robots do these tasks at a rate of 75 to 125 cookies a minute.

While industrial robots are characterized by their use in factories, service robots are mobile, uncontained, and extremely diverse. Police and fire departments, and especially the military, use robotic machines extensively to operate in hazardous locations where humans are at risk. More and more, domestic robots perform cleaning and maintenance in our homes and workplaces. There are many jobs humans would rather leave to robots. A task may be boring, such as domestic cleaning, or dangerous, such as exploring a volcano. Other jobs are physically inaccessible, such as exploring another planet, cleaning the inside of a long pipe, or performing surgery. Almost every unmanned space probe ever launched was a robot.

The advent of service robots for personal human use is a new development in the 21st century. McDonald's has been testing a high-tech grill complete with a robotic burger-flipping machine. Some robot makers are trying out companion robots that scoot around long-term care communities and hospitals. Rigged with a video screen and camera, they allow two-way telecom links between patients, nurses, and off-site physicians. Shoppers may soon encounter warehouse stores,

(continues on page 20)

Automobile Manufacturing

Robots used in the automotive industry range from crash test dummies to assembly line machines that lift engines and other heavy loads. Robots even tow finished vehicles out of the plant and park them to await loading for transportation. Most automotive industry robots, however, are relatively simple articulated arms that perform riveting, screwing, bolt tightening, and welding duties. The automobile industry began using robots in the manufacturing process to increase production and profits. Although robots have assumed duties once performed by people, they still require frequent maintenance and calibration. Humans still need to monitor safety and productivity issues. Robots are used for most heavy lifting and precision work, but humans do the finishing work and inspections. There are some robot jobs, such as automobile safety and crashworthiness testing, that no human would apply for. Imagine being shot at a brick wall in a car at 120 miles per hour (193 km/hr), just to see how the impact affects your body and then repeating the test under thousands of different scenarios.

A typical automotive assembly plant is divided into three major sections. In the first, exterior body panels and the interior frame are assembled and welded together. This work is mostly performed by robots, but may also require some manual welding. During this stage, the body is attached to a conveyor system that will move it through the entire assembly process. Throughout the process, numerous inspections are performed by robots and humans to ensure the quality of the work. The painting process occupies the second section of the assembly plant, where bodies of cars pass through a series of paint rooms. Here, the bodies are dipped into chemicals to prevent rust and seal the metal. Then the components are primed, painted, and sealed with a clear coat. Final assembly of the vehicle takes place in the third section. Here, parts such as the seats, dashboard, engine, and transmission are installed. Although machines assist with loading heavy parts, much of the assembly work is still performed by team assemblers working with power tools.

One challenge related to robotic car assembly includes determining if new components will fit into the car assembly and then finding the most efficient way for the robot to install the component. New computer-assisted design software

10011101001010101001100101110110101001010101

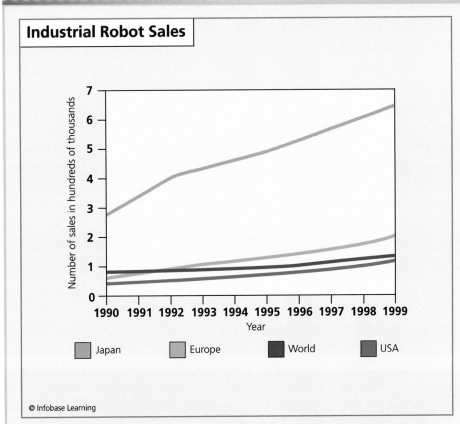

Industrial Robot Sales

© Infobase Learning

Industrial robots are now used routinely for welding, to manufacture automobiles, and to inspect and test products. The replacement of human workers by robots to perform certain tasks represents the culmination of the mechanization of work initiated by Henry Ford, Frederick Taylor, and others in the efficiency movement in the early 20th century.

can perform virtual installation of car components, detecting when problems will occur and offering advice on how the component should be redesigned. The software is also capable of simulating flexibility in components, factoring the amount of bend in the component into assembly planning. The interactive program allows changes to components to be applied and previewed in a matter of seconds.

10011101001010101001100101110110101001010101

(continued from page 17)

such as Costco or Home Depot, where robots are shelving items. As prices fall and robots become more autonomous, simple robots dedicated to a single task may work in more than a million homes. They will handle simple but unwanted jobs, such as vacuum cleaning, floor washing, and lawn mowing. Many consumers have taken home one of iRobot's popular Roomba machines, small robot vacuum cleaners that can navigate around a room, cleaning as they go.

When a human cannot be present on site to perform a job because it is dangerous, faraway, or inaccessible, *teleoperated robots,* or *telerobots,* are used. Rather than following a predetermined sequence of movements, a telerobot is controlled from a distance by a human operator. The robot may be in another room or another country or on a very different scale to the operator. For instance, a *laparoscopic surgery* robot can enter a patient's body via a small probe placed through a tiny incision, significantly shortening recovery time in comparison to traditional surgery. A member of a bomb squad can send a small robot to disable a bomb. Telerobot aircraft are increasingly being used by the United States military, notably in remote, dangerous regions like Afghanistan. These pilotless drones can search terrain and fire on targets.

Robots have a competitive advantage over humans in some areas: they can perform some tasks more quickly and efficiently than a human worker; they never get sick or need to rest; they make precise, continuous movements; and they are not bored by repetitive and unrewarding work. Humans, however, gain some ground back in other areas: Robots are not creative or innovative and do not think independently. They are unable to make complicated decisions and cannot learn from their mistakes. They do not adapt well to changes in their surroundings. In the end, every successful business must depend on people for these abilities.

AUTOMATIC PROCESS CONTROL

Process control refers to the regulation of mechanical systems. *Automatic process control* uses computer technology and software engineering to help power plants and factories in industries as diverse as paper, mining, and cement operate more efficiently and safely. In theory, a controller could be used for any process that has a measurable output, a known ideal value for that output, and a control mechanism. Controllers are used in industry to regulate temperature, pressure, flow rate, chemical composition, speed, and practically every other variable for which a measurement exists. For example, such systems can perform the following:

- detect dangerous conditions, such as high temperatures in the core of a nuclear power plant, and sound alarms in response
- decide when to open and close valves to control the flow of water and other substances
- decide when to order new fuel and components
- decide when machinery needs to be serviced

Automated process control systems are used to increase the quality, speed, and safety of industrial processes. The workers here are using process control software to monitor the production of a computer circuit board. *(Tom Raymond/Stone/Getty Images)*

In the absence of process automation, plant operators have to physically monitor performance values and the quality of outputs to determine the best settings on which to run production equipment. Maintenance is carried out at set intervals. This can lead to operational inefficiency and unsafe operating conditions.

Process automation simplifies this with the help of sensors at thousands of spots around the plant that collect data on temperatures, pressures, flows, and other process variables. The information is stored and analyzed on a computer, and the entire plant and each piece of production equipment can be monitored on a large screen in a control room. Plant operating settings are then automatically adjusted to achieve the optimum production. Plant operators can manually override the process automation systems when necessary.

QUALITY ASSURANCE

Quality assurance (QA), is the systematic process of testing products such as machines and software before they are sold to ensure that they are free from flaws. QA cannot absolutely guarantee the production of quality products, but it can maximize the probability that minimum standards are being attained by the production process. QA is not limited to manufacturing and can be applied to any business or nonbusiness activity. It has become a popular concept across many fields in recent years. Some of those include administrative services, banking, computer software development, retailing, transportation, and education.

Design verification and quality assurance processes are the backbone of successful product development. Whatever the product, the ultimate goals are the same: to reduce development costs and accelerate time to market without affecting product quality. Companies invest considerable time, resources, and money in QA testing. To reduce test development time and improve test coverage and efficiency, many companies have created automated testing systems.

Stress testing, or failure testing, is the process of using a product until it fails, often under stresses such as increasing vibration, temperature, or humidity. This testing can expose unanticipated weaknesses in a product, and the data obtained are used to drive engineering and manufacturing improvements. *Software quality assurance (SQA)* uses automated processes as a means of checking the functionality of code and scanning for errors.

001101010010100111010110101010101011001010000

Integrated Circuit Fabrication

In electronics, an *integrated circuit (IC),* also known as a chip or microchip, is a miniaturized electronic circuit that has been manufactured in the surface of a thin substrate of semiconductor material. Integrated circuits are used in almost all electronic equipment in use today and have revolutionized the world of electronics. Computers, mobile phones, and other digital appliances are now inextricable parts of the structure of modern societies, and all are made possible by the low production cost of integrated circuits.

Integrated circuits are now manufactured almost entirely automatically. The integration of large numbers of tiny *transistors* into a small chip was an enormous improvement over the manual assembly of circuits using electronic components. The integrated circuit's mass production capability, reliability, and building-block approach to circuit design ensured the rapid adoption of standardized circuits. They replaced *discrete circuits,* which are electronic circuits that contain separate components, such as resistors and transistors, instead of a single integrated circuit. ICs have two main advantages over discrete circuits: cost and performance. Cost is low because the chips, with all their components, are printed as a unit by *photolithography* rather than being constructed one transistor at a time. ICs also require much less building material. Performance is high since the compact, close-packed components switch quickly and consume little power compared to their discrete counterparts.

Early versions of the integrated circuit go back to 1949, when the German engineer Werner Jacobi filed a patent for a device with five transistors on a common substrate. Jacobi listed hearing aids as a typical industrial application for his patent. Perfecting the manufacture of the semiconducting material took decades of research and development. Semiconductor device fabrication is a multiple-step sequence of photographic and chemical processing steps during which electronic circuits are gradually created on a wafer of semiconducting material. The wafers are most often made of silicon, although other materials are used for specialized applications, such as lasers and solar cells.

The entire manufacturing process takes six to eight weeks and is performed in highly specialized facilities. Intel, the world's largest microchip manufacturer,

(continues)

001101010010100111010110101010101011001010000

0011010100101001110101101010101011001010000

(continued)

has facilities in Europe and Asia as well as the United States. In 2005, a fabrication facility cost more than $1 billion to build, because so much of the operation was automated. Many toxic materials are used in the fabrication process, and it is vital that workers not be directly exposed to these substances. The high degree of automation helps reduce the risks of exposure. Most fabrication facilities also employ sophisticated exhaust management systems to control the risk to workers and the environment.

0011010100101001110101101010101011001010000

Some companies make their testing processes a selling point. Shoppers in IKEA home goods stores have probably seen one of their sales-floor demonstrations of durability—a robotic arm mounted on a display pushes down on an armchair over and over again.

THREE-DIMENSIONAL PRINTING

A *digital fabricator* (sometimes shortened to fabber and sometimes called a 3-D printer) is a small, self-contained factory that can make objects described by digital data. These devices work on the same principles as a printer for an average desktop computer and make three-dimensional (3-D), solid objects that can be used as models, prototypes, or deliverable products.

A 3-D printer works by translating a computer scan of an object into a series of extremely thin cross-sectional slices. Each slice is then printed one on top of the other to create a three-dimensional replica of the original object. Although many different technologies are available for 3-D printing, inkjet 3-D printing is increasingly preferred for its speed, low cost, and ease of use. Its applications include prototype production, metal casting, architecture, education, and health care. Other uses include reconstructing fossils in paleontology, replicating ancient and priceless archaeological artifacts, and reconstructing bones and body parts in forensic pathology. This printing technology is also being studied by biotechnology firms and medical researchers for possible use in tissue engineering applications. Pioneering researchers are seeking ways to build viable organs and body parts with

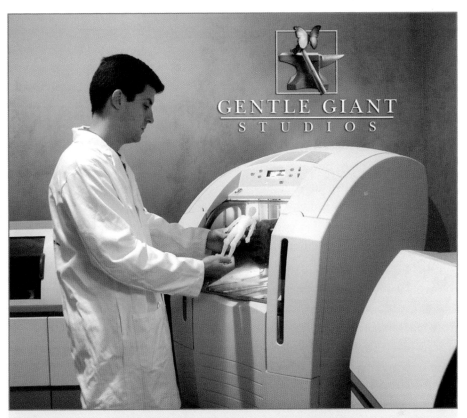

Three-dimensional printers, also called fabricators, can produce real-life products automatically, based on digital representations of those products. For example, an engineer can use computer-aided design (CAD) software to create a three-dimensional model of a screw, and then use a three-dimensional printer to "print" a model of that screw, usually constructed from plastic. *(InVision 3D printer by 3D Systems Corp.; Getty Images)*

inkjet techniques that deposit layers of living cells onto a gel medium to form working 3-D structures. A prototype kidney can be produced in about seven hours.

Even do-it-yourselfers are experimenting with this technology, as open source hardware designs and relatively affordable printer setups become available. One model, called the Makerbot, costs less than $1,000 for a build-your-own kit. Users can feed in two kinds of plastics: ABS, the same material Lego bricks are made of, and HDPE, which is used in milk jugs. Makerbot can create objects up to four by four by six inches; some available designs include iPod docks, bracelets, and hair clips.

MASS CUSTOMIZATION

Once, every man-made item was unique in some way. Craftspeople made their products by hand, and as a result no finished piece was exactly the same as any other. Today, this quality is prized and can command a hefty price. But when the industrial age arrived, technology made mass manufacturing possible. A single design for a product could be turned into thousands or millions of exact copies. Factory-made objects were inexpensive and reliable. If a part broke, it was simple to order a new one and replace it.

However, the downside of mass manufacturing is that products are no longer tailored to consumers' individual needs. Instead, to maximize profit, companies tend to create products that appeal to the lowest common denominator. Products have lost their individualized appeal, utility, and charm. Mass customization, the process of enabling people to buy automatically manufactured products that are customized to their preferences, is in part an attempt to combine the best of the old and new worlds. It merges the cost savings and rapid production from mass manufacturing and the individual customization from old-fashioned artisan-based construction to create an alternative that gives customers a dazzling array of choices.

The evolution of the clothing industry illustrates the journey from craft production to mass production and sketches out the future potential of mass customization. Prior to the 1800s, clothing items were acquired by making them at home or by placing an order with a tailor or seamstress. Francis C. Lowell (1775–1817) introduced the power loom to the New England cotton industry in 1813. Although it would take another decade of improvements to increase the speed and accuracy of the machine, Lowell's innovation eventually produced commercially accepted, good-quality cloth. By about 1860, clothing manufacturers started using sewing machines, which made a wider variety of clothing items faster and cheaper to produce. And in 1863, Ebenezer Butterick and his wife introduced the paper pattern. What this meant to the apparel industry was that rather than having to create an original garment to serve as a pattern, they could use inexpensive paper. This development also allowed the standardization of sizes.

It became standard practice for manufacturers to divide a garment into sections and assign each section to an individual worker. Sometimes these workers were in factories, and sometimes they were individuals working from home. In essence, this division of labor transformed the production of clothing into an assembly line. As a result of technological innovations, as well as the simplification of fashion styles and an increase in the number of women working outside the home, the industry of ready-made clothing was well established in America by 1910.

Technology continues to change the industry in a variety of ways. Computerized tracking allows manufacturers to lower inventory and create a larger profit margin by decreasing the number of unsold products. Digital technology is playing a role in this movement as well, and returning the element of customization that was lost when Lowell introduced the power loom. Now the customer can be involved in product design. Instead of mass-producing generic objects for a broad target audience, computer technology has erased the expectation that customization must always carry a high price. Internet marketing and distribution enables designers to target custom-designed products to niche communities and individuals.

A visit to the Nike Web site, for example, allows customers to choose one of several athletic shoe styles and customize it with a rainbow of colors and other design options. Gemvara, an online jewelry company, allows customers to choose from a range of customizable designs. Once a customer has clicked through her options for gemstones, settings, and metals, the piece is made to order.

Mass customization generally follows one of five approaches described by researchers—popularizing, varietizing, accessorizing, parametering, and tailoring:

- *Popularizing* is when the manufacturer offers a customer a limited product line. Apple has done this with its iPhone and iPad lines. The range of choices is fairly narrow, although Apple regularly introduces upgraded models.
- *Varietizing* can be thought of as changing the color of the product the customer wants to order. The products are all the same, but if five dresses are offered in 10 colors each, the customer has 50 options. The choices available to consumers have changed quite a bit since 1923, when Henry Ford famously said, "Any customer can have a car painted any color that he wants so long as it is black."
- *Accessorizing* allows the customer to add features to a core product. An example would be the cases customers can purchase for their

iPhones or the applications and games they can buy from Apple's App Store.

- *Parametering* is the model Dell uses to provide customers with a customized personal computer. Customers select the features they want and the computer maker tells them what hardware they should order to create their final product.
- *Tailoring* invites the customer to provide product specifications from the beginning of the manufacturing process.

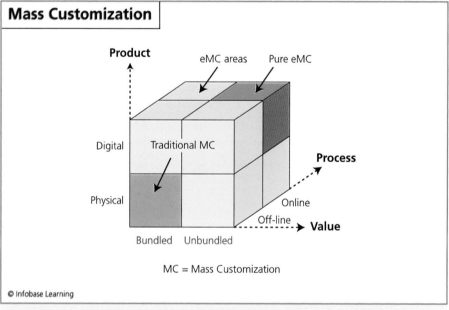

Mass Customization

MC = Mass Customization

© Infobase Learning

The 20th century saw the rise of mass manufacturing where individual products were manufactured in large quantities and sold to the public. Although mass manufacturing made it possible to reduce the price of products ranging from clothing to appliances to medical devices, one disadvantage of mass manufacturing is that all copies of any product are identical. Mass customization seeks to provide consumers with the ability to customize products to suit their preferences, without sacrificing the low cost and speed of mass manufacturing. This diagram illustrates how a mass customization market can vary in the form of the product (either physical or digital), in its value (either bundled or unbundled with a physical medium), and in the nature of the customization process (either offline or online). A business that takes telephone orders for customized personal computers is an example of physical, bundled, and offline mass customization, while a Web site that enables users to generate their own ringtones for download onto their smartphones is an example of digital, unbundled, and online mass customization.

`100111010010101010011001011101101010010101001`

John Henry, Mythical Worker Defeated by a Steam-Powered Hammer

The tale of John Henry is known through story, song, and cartoon. A powerful steel driver, John Henry worked for the Chesapeake and Ohio (C&O) Railway, chiseling tunnels through the rock with a steel drill to make way for the railroad tracks from Chesapeake Bay to the Ohio Valley through the Allegheny Mountains. When the Big Bend Mountain rose in the way of the tracks, the railroad workers were told to build through it, as the mountain was too big to build around. A thousand men worked tirelessly for three years to accomplish the task, with hundreds of lives lost to the treacherous mountain.

A statue of John Henry alongside State Highway 12, south of Talcott, West Virginia. The statue is placed above the Big Bend tunnel on the C & O Railroad where many believe the man vs. machine competition originally took place. *(Ken Thomas)*

John Henry emerged as the most powerful steel driver working for the railroad, wielding a 14-pound hammer to bash through 10 to 20 feet of rock during a single workday. One day, a salesman came to the railroad management, boasting that a steam-powered machine could drill more efficiently than any man working on the tracks. John Henry challenged the steam hammer to a race and won, driving 14 feet to the steam hammer's nine. But exhausted by the task, John Henry collapsed and died immediately after his victory.

Historians have long explored the possibility of John Henry's existence outside the folk legend. Some have concluded that John Henry was a former slave, freed by the Civil War. Scott Reynolds Nelson speculates in *Steel Drivin' Man: John Henry: The Untold Story of an American Legend* (2006) that John William Henry was a former Union soldier, arrested for theft, convicted and leased

(continues)

`100111010010101010011001011101101010010101001`

(continued)

out to the railroad company along with other inmates from the Virginia State Penitentiary. Nelson, an associate professor of history at the College of William and Mary in Williamsburg, Virginia, came across multiple records of convicts working for railways while in the process of gathering information for a study of southern railroads during Reconstruction. Large numbers of convicts were leased out to the C&O Railway in the late 1800s as a source of prison revenue, working for as little as 25 cents a day.

A few lines from one of many John Henry ballads describing his burial in the sand near a white house suggested to Nelson that John Henry could have been a convict, for the walls of the Virginia State Penitentiary were white. In 1992, workers demolishing the penitentiary uncovered a few hundred skeletons buried near the walls, further confirming Nelson's theory and the possibility that John Henry could have been buried there. A thorough examination of the Virginia state archives yielded a possible match. Henry's disappearance from all prison records by 1874 suggests that he was neither released nor paroled, for there would have been a record, but that he died outside the prison walls and his death went unrecorded.

Although the John Henry songs refer to the Big Bend Tunnel as the site of the competition between the man and the steam hammer, Nelson, who traveled to examine the Big Bend tunnel in West Virginia, concluded that it was not likely. The rock there was too soft to require steam drills, and the mountain passages were too narrow to accommodate them. John William Henry was sent to work on the Lewis Tunnel, also in West Virginia, where steam drills were used alongside human drillers. The early steam drills used in this period, although powerful, broke often and easily and were not very efficient. They were, however, highly efficient in generating lots of silicone dust. When inhaled, the dust can cause silicosis, a severe and often fatal lung disease that was common among railroad workers. John Henry's collapse and death could have been a result of silicosis, rather than exhaustion or a failed heart.

Although the historical evidence unearthed by Nelson is by no means certain, it provides some support for the mythical steel drivin' man and continues to fuel the story of a powerful working class hero.

Nearly all business expenses fall into two broad categories—fixed and marginal. Fixed costs include setting up plants, installing equipment, and hiring workers. These costs are incurred before the first sale is made. Marginal costs, on the other hand, come after an enterprise is up and running. They cover the expenses of producing additional units of output, including wages, raw materials, electricity, marketing, and distribution. Mass customization becomes optimal when both fixed and marginal costs—particularly fixed—are low.

Modern technologies slash fixed costs in three areas: information, production, and distribution. By making it easy to supply information, the Internet gives consumers a cheap and easy way to find out which goods and services are available. Companies can display immense amounts of product information on their Web pages and take orders from anywhere in the world. The Internet also reduces the cost to producers of gathering information about what buyers want. Even assembly lines are no longer limited to endless repetitions of the same product. Computer-aided designs are replacing costly prototypes, and computer-guided machinery allows production to shift among styles with a few lines of computer code, significantly reducing the time and expense of retooling. Improvements in distribution reduce the costs of delivering products to consumers. As the Internet spreads into more places, the cost of delivering information products will continue to drop by orders of magnitude.

Interestingly, craft manufacturing is also enjoying an Internet-fueled renaissance. Etsy, an e-commerce site where artisans sell their creations, had 2 million buyers last year. They spent a total of $90 million dollars as part of a larger trend called micro-manufacturing. Consumers still crave the charm and individuality of handmade items, and the Internet makes them easily accessible and affordable.

CONCLUSIONS

People have always feared that once machines were used to perform human tasks humans would eventually be replaced by machines. As the inventor Rotwang in Fritz Lang's 1927 classic science fiction film *Metropolis* declared, "I have created a machine in the image of a man, that never tires or makes a mistake. Now we have no further use for living workers."

Such concerns have a legitimate basis. Technological obsolescence, automation, and outsourcing have all put pressures on employees in recent years to upgrade their skills or join the ranks of the unemployed. Although some believe that it will never be possible to automate jobs requiring creativity, many who held this belief in the past have turned out to be wrong. The crafts once practiced by the blacksmith, millwright, and tanner were all considered to require expert human skill at one time, but now have been almost entirely replaced by machines.

Yet in recent years, there has been some reversal in this trend, largely as a result of computers, the Internet, and automated manufacturing technology. Individual craftspeople who make clothing, jewelry, and furniture were once limited to marketing their wares at small local craft fairs, but now can advertise nationwide and even worldwide by taking advantage of eBay, Amazon, Etsy, and other Internet marketing channels. As a result, it is becoming increasingly possible for craftspeople who design and make niche products—those that appeal only to a small segment of the population—to sell a high enough volume of those products to make the enterprise worthwhile. Because their production costs are low, such craftspeople do not need to sell millions of their products to make a profit, as a traditional mass manufacturer would need to do. Chris Anderson, the editor of *Wired* magazine, has referred to this phenomenon, in which a large number of producers sell a relatively small number of units of a large number of products to a large number of consumers, as the long tail, in an allusion to the shape of the graph that illustrates the sales of both mass-manufactured products and individually manufactured products.

The decreasing cost of 3-D printers to manufacture individual copies of a product on demand is making it even easier and less expensive to design and sell a product in small quantities and still make a profit. As such printers become more widespread, they will likely be used to print products at a location that is as close as possible to the buyer, thereby reducing shipping costs to a minimum.

In the end, therefore, although some fears about the replacement of people by robots have been justified, at the dawn of the 21st century there are strong signs that humans are taking back the reins and leveraging robots to recreate cottage industries run by artisans, only with the town market and covered wagon replaced by the Internet and FedEx as their marketing and distribution departments.

3

ADMINISTRATIVE ASSISTANTS: FROM TYPIST TO OFFICE MANAGER

The role of an administrative assistant is to ensure that the supervisor can accomplish his or her job as efficiently and effectively as possible and to allow the supervisor to focus only on those tasks that require his or her skills to perform. Although this general description of the job function performed by an administrative assistant have remained unchanged over time, the specific skills required by administrative assistants have changed significantly, as computers and the Internet have made it possible to perform some tasks without any human intervention and to perform other tasks more quickly and with less human skill than ever before. This chapter explores the history of administrative assistants, examines the ways in which the responsibilities and skills of administrative assistants today differ from those of yesterday, and explains how modern administrative assistants use computers and the Internet to support the work of their supervisors.

ADMINISTRATIVE ASSISTANTS BEFORE COMPUTERS

The job description for a typical administrative assistant today covers a wide variety of tasks. They handle administrative details for company projects and coordinate work flow. An assistant might compose correspondence and reports for a manager, manage a departmental budget, answer and sort e-mail, handle phone inquiries, provide backup materials for teleconferences, set up meetings, and arrange travel logistics. An assistant must ensure discretion and control interruptions. Daily routines might include reordering supplies, updating mail and phone directories, and training or supervising other secretarial or clerical staff. As recently as a generation or two ago, that description would have been quite different and much more limited. Responsibilities might have included the following:

- taking dictation, then typing—manually—letters and other documents
- retyping multiple copies of the same document—remember, copy machines and printers did not yet exist
- keeping the boss's calendar on paper
- opening, sorting, and reading the boss's mail
- making travel arrangements, possibly by going to the train station or calling the travel agent
- writing out paper checks to be signed by the boss
- running personal errands for the boss

Some of those responsibilities have been made obsolete by computers. Changes in technology have also created new job duties, such as managing budgets, that administrative assistants of the past did not handle. In fact, some of those high-level responsibilities would have been spread across multiple people, such as an office manager, travel agent, and bookkeeper. Now all are commonly handled by a single administrative assistant.

The growth of office technology, culminating with today's computers and Internet connections, radically changed the duties of office workers. Writer Deb Ng describes her first job in 1985 when she was a 20-year-old receptionist: "My desk was in the front of the suite of offices just before the elevators. To the right of my desk was an IBM Selectric typewriter, but my desk itself was clear save for some filing and a pad for messages. I prided myself on my neat handwriting, one of the things that helped me to land the job, and I manually wrote message after message onto the pad. Every now and then I would get up and deliver messages to their respective parties."

The table on the following page contrasts a few administrative routines from a few decades ago with today's typical office.

Office surroundings have evolved as well. Initially, they were affected by the same changes that swept American industry in the late 1800s, when Frederick

ADMINISTRATIVE ASSISTANTS: YESTERDAY AND TODAY

Task	Office of Yesterday	Office of Today
Typing letters or memos	The assistant would use a typewriter. If she made a mistake she could use correcting fluid or, on a state-of-the-art electric typewriter, backspace to use the erasing tape. Too many mistakes would mean starting over with a clean sheet of paper.	The assistant uses a word processing program on her desktop or laptop computer. Automatic spell-checking helps catch mistakes, and the edited and revised document can be printed cleanly.
Making copies	The assistant would type multiple copies of documents or possibly layer pages with messy sheets of carbon paper that were carefully rolled into the typewriter.	Printers and copy machines have taken over this task.
Keeping in touch with customers and clients	The assistant would use the phone. First thing every morning, she would retrieve hand-written messages from the receptionist and spend an hour or two getting back to people	E-mail, voice mail, and text messages keep colleagues and customers in constant contact. Groups of colleagues can hold virtual meetings with live audio and video.
Telecommuting	Did not exist, although workers might take home paper copies to proofread or an occasional file to go over.	An assistant might use an Internet connection to work from home a few days a week or perhaps from a location entirely remote from the main office.
Making payments or delivering contracts	Offices relied on snail mail—actual letters written on actual stationery. It could take several days to send paperwork to someone. Overnight delivery was very expensive and was used only for urgent matters. Fax machines came into wide use in the 1980s, but documents requiring an original signature still had to go through the postal service.	E-mail and faxes send documents almost instantaneously. Scanners and digital signatures have replaced the need for physical signatures in many cases. When they have not, overnight delivery has become much more affordable.
Ordering supplies	The assistant would fill out and mail a catalog order form. Faster orders were placed by phone.	Online ordering sends supplies on their way with a few mouse clicks.
Reviewing and updating budgets	Would have been handled by a bookkeeper.	Handled with a spreadsheet program such as Microsoft Excel.

Taylor developed his scientific management techniques that taught factory managers to save money and increase productivity by making their employees more efficient. Taylor's principles divided skills into a sequence of simple procedures to be taught to workers and monitored by management.

Scientific management's success in industry led to its adoption in the office. Soon there were clerks who only opened letters, clerks who only typed, clerks who only filed, and couriers who picked up and delivered files from one person to the next. Typists did not take shorthand; stenographers did not file. Theoretically, valuable company time would be wasted if a stenographer left her desk to file. Individual approaches to tasks were discouraged. Job standardization made it easy for managers to keep a close eye on work flow, counting typists' strokes or the number of letters opened per hour. Offices were open spaces without partitions, where workers could easily be monitored. Workers were not allowed to talk, because conversation cut into work time. By the 1920s, the office, like the factory, was tedious and stressful for the worker and closely monitored by the manager.

When World War II ended, American industry tooled up to satisfy pent-up demand for consumer goods after the long war years of scarcity. Factory jobs were suddenly paying far more than office jobs, so employers had to make office work more attractive. Instead of increasing clerical salaries, however, management emphasized the status of office work. Scientific management was modified to make jobs less routine, and the look of the office began to change to outwardly show this functional change. Advertisements for jobs described friendly offices. Attractive health insurance and retirement plans became part of the financial rewards for working. Physically, offices became color coordinated with comfortable and attractive furniture. For many workers, their office environment was far more luxurious than their homes. Today's workplace design is no longer dictated by the product or service produced; nor is it a matter of simply looking good. Rather, it is driven by increased competition, rapid technological advances, and economic shifts. Where it was once important to have impressive offices—often intended to convey a company's prestige—the current trend is toward modest facilities, which also save corporations money. An estimated 40 million Americans, nearly 60 percent of the white-collar workforce, work in cubicles. Not everyone appreciates the office cubicle culture. Some workers feel uncomfortable without doors that they can close, and although an open office facilitates communication, it can also create distractions.

Technology has also had a significant impact on the design of the workplace. Desktop computers have replaced typewriters, adding machines, and file cabinets. E-mail and voice mail have all but eliminated the stackable in-box and pink telephone message slips. The result is lower overhead, less clutter, and higher worker productivity. Many office computers are networked, enabling employees to share files and resources. Many of these desktop systems are connected to other offices via *intranets* and with systems around the world via the Internet. Networking fosters rapid communication, enables collaboration among workers regardless of geography, and permits access to the wealth of information posted on the World Wide Web.

Changes in society, such as a more mobile workforce and workers' demands for flexibility, have fueled the development of portable office equipment. Laptop computers and cellular phones now equip a growing telecommuting workforce and, in some cases, have eliminated the need for central offices altogether. In addition, a ready supply of independent contractors, many of whom maintain fully equipped home offices, has enabled many businesses to employ independent contractors and other *freelancers* for tasks that previously would have required hiring more staff and purchasing specialized equipment. The cost savings for many of these companies can be substantial.

WORD PROCESSORS

The history of modern office automation began with the typewriter and the copy machine, which mechanized once-manual tasks. Increasingly, automation involves not just the mechanization of tasks but the conversion of information to electronic form as well. The term *word processing* was invented by IBM in the late 1960s. It originally referred to any machine that processed words, such as dictating machines and ordinary electric typewriters. By the early 1970s, however, the term generally referred to typewriters with some form of electronic editing and correction ability and the capacity to produce perfect originals. Although features and design varied, word processors usually featured a monochrome display and the ability to save documents on *diskettes*. Later models introduced innovations such as spell-checking programs, formatting options, and *dot-matrix printing*. As the more versatile combination of a personal computer and separate printer became commonplace, most business-machine companies stopped manufacturing the word processor as a stand-alone office machine. Word processing was one of the earliest applications for the personal computer in office productivity. MacWrite, Microsoft Works, and other software for the Apple Macintosh, introduced in 1984, were probably the first true *what you see is what you get (WYSIWYG)* word processors until the introduction of Microsoft Windows. Dedicated word processors eventually became museum pieces.

This technological advance came with major implications for office workers. In 1971, a third of all working women in the United States were secretaries. Some manufacturers, according to a *New York Times* article that year, claimed "the concept of word processing" would replace the traditional secretary and give women new administrative roles in business and industry. But the National Secretaries Association feared that word processing would transform secretaries into "space-age typing pools." The article considered only the organizational changes resulting from secretaries' operating word processors rather than typewriters. The possibility that word processors might lead to managers creating documents without the intervention of secretaries was not considered.

Although word processors have changed the role of administrative assistants in the process of document creation and editing, human administrative assistants are still needed to perform some tasks.

- Spell-checking. Computer spell-checkers get better all the time, but they still cannot be relied upon for everything. For example, names, technical terms, and industry-specific jargon often do not appear in the dictionaries of word processors. Human administrative assistants need to know how to handle such terms. Further, spell-checkers cannot detect when a correctly spelled word is not the proper word to use. For example, a computer might not flag the sentence, "I will see you their."
- Correct names and addresses. Only a human can detect whether a letter, memo, or other document is addressed to the correct recipient. Sending information to the wrong people could result in revealing confidential information to the wrong person or failing to provide information to someone who needs it.
- Electronic v. paper formatting. Although modern word processors display documents in a format very similar to their printed version, differences still crop up. If a document in its final form is to be delivered on paper, the document must be printed and proofread on

Typewriter v. Word Processor Workflow

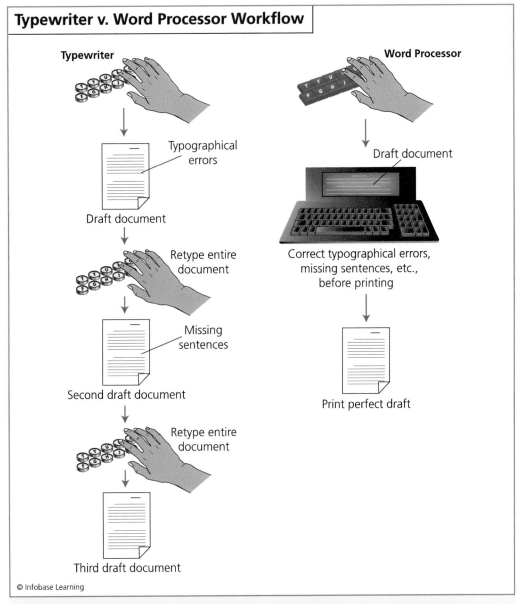

© Infobase Learning

Switching from a typewriter to a word processor to write a document does not only enable the author to type more quickly. Authoring a document using a word processor can also enable one to write more efficiently by eliminating the need to retype the entire document multiple times merely to correct typographical errors, insert additional sentences, and make other changes.

paper to catch errors that cannot be found on-screen. For example, if a document contains a font that is not stored on the printer, characters may appear incorrectly once printed. A human is needed to

Document Management Systems

A *document management system* controls the life cycle of documents in an organization—how they are created, reviewed, and published, and how they are ultimately disposed of or retained. Such systems make documents easy to find, because they are organized according to metadata such as author, creation date, project name, client, etc. The systems also provide security, because different access rights can be granted depending on people's needs. For example, only employees in the accounting department may be granted access to financial documents, while all employees may be granted access to information about company holidays and health benefits.

The systems can give many people within an organization access to documents, eliminating problems with *shared hard drives* that may not be shared across the entire organization. Also, shared hard drives can be problematic because giving employees direct access to them can also give them the ability to tamper, intentionally or not, with other software on the hard drive. In contrast, when users are given access to a document management system but not to any shared hard drives, they can only access documents and not any other files on the server.

Many document management systems also have a *check-out/check-in* feature, so if one person is editing a document, no one else can make changes until the first person has finished, eliminating the possibility of creating two inconsistent versions of the same document. Another common feature is the ability to perform document assembly using databases. This lets employees easily create commonly used form letters by having the document management system automatically fill in data such as the recipient's name and address, a deadline for response, and the name of the person signing the document.

An effective document management system specifies:

- What types of documents and other content can be created
- What template to use for each type of document
- What metadata to provide for each type of document

check for such problems by reviewing the entire printed document and not assume that because the electronic document was proofread that the paper document does not need to be.

- ⊕ Where to store a document at each stage of its life cycle
- ⊕ How to control access to a document at each stage of its life cycle
- ⊕ How to move documents within the organization as team members contribute to the documents' creation, review, approval, publication, and disposition
- ⊕ What policies to apply to documents so that document-related actions are audited, documents are retained or disposed of properly, and content that is important to the organization is protected
- ⊕ How documents are treated as corporate records, which must be retained according to legal requirements and corporate guidelines

Microsoft's *SharePoint* is a leader in the document management system market, and IBM and Google have released their own systems. A quick search will turn up dozens of other options, from comprehensive customized solutions to freely available open source software. Cloud-based services have burst onto the market with products suited to just about any document management need, from individual users' personal files to multinational organizations that must follow document retention regulations. Because cloud providers have huge economies of scale, they can deliver virtually unlimited storage capacity at very low prices, including the ability to back up documents to geographically diverse repositories. The free Google Docs service is perhaps the best known of these, offering basic features such as shared editing, version control, content indexing, and all management headaches handed off to someone else. But other players, such as Microsoft's SharePoint Online, are steadily entering the market.

The advantage of these systems is low cost of entry: They require nothing more than a Web browser to get started. Cloud-based document management does have some vulnerabilities, such as dependence on the Internet. Users should weigh reliability carefully before committing their most mission-critical document management processes to the cloud. Another potential problem is security. Cloud users must trust that their provider is adequately protecting proprietary data using encryption and multiple layers of defense.

Administrative assistants have also taken on new responsibilities in the document creation and editing process. They design templates and update them in response to changes. Certain documents must contain particular information or be formatted according to particular requirements. For example, legal documents submitted to a court may be required to have page numbers on the bottom of every page and be signed on the final page. Although the attorney who writes such documents is ultimately responsible for ensuring that they meet requirements, this responsibility typically falls to an administrative assistant. In fact, an experienced legal secretary may have more knowledge in this area than many attorneys.

Administrative assistants are still needed for creating and editing documents. Although they do less straight typing than in the past, they are still on the front lines of ensuring quality and accuracy. Much of what they do now involves reading, understanding, and editing documents rather than merely reproducing what others have said or written. Their jobs have become more cognitively demanding and perhaps also more fulfilling.

AUTOMATIC SPEECH RECOGNITION

People have been developing mechanical means of recording and transmitting the human voice for more than a century. In 1881, Alexander Graham Bell (1847–1922), his cousin Chichester Bell (1848–1924), and Charles Sumner Tainter (1854–1940) invented a recording device with a rotating wax-coated cylinder on which grooves could be cut by a stylus that responded to incoming sound pressure in much the same way as a microphone that Bell invented earlier for use with the telephone.

Based on this invention, Bell and Tainter formed the Volta Graphophone Co. in 1888 to manufacture machines for the recording and reproduction of sound in office environments. The American Graphophone Co., which later became the Columbia Graphophone Co., acquired the patent in 1907 and trademarked the term *Dictaphone.* Around the same time, Thomas Edison invented the *phonograph* using a tinfoil-based cylinder, which was subsequently adapted to wax. His Ediphone competed directly with Columbia. The purpose of these products was to record dictation of notes and letters for a secretary who would later type them, thereby circumventing the need for costly stenographers.

This turn-of-the-century concept of office mechanization spawned a range of electronic implements and improvements, including the electric typewriter. It takes little imagination to envision the obvious interest in creating an automatic typewriter that could directly transcribe a human voice without having to deal with the annoyance of recording and handling the speech on wax cylinders or other recording media.

A similar kind of automation took place a century later in the 1990s with the advent of *call centers*. One example of such a service was the AT&T Operator Line, which helped a caller place calls, arrange payment methods, and conduct credit card transactions. The number of work stations in a large call center could reach several thousand. *Automatic speech recognition* technologies provided the capability of automating some call handling functions, reducing the large operating cost of a call center. The AT&T Voice Recognition Call Processing service, introduced in 1992, routinely handles about 1.2 billion voice transactions with machines each year using automatic speech recognition technology to appropriately route and handle the calls.

Automatic speech recognition by computer, in real time and using only an input audio signal, has developed over the last two decades to the point where it is useful for a number of practical applications, such as telephone enquiry services and office dictation. Modern systems have almost entirely eliminated taking dictation as a job task for administrative assistants. The efficiency of automated dictation has improved dramatically. Note taking or handwriting is 20 or 30 words per minute (wpm); typing is typically 40–60 wpm; and computerized note taking and summary systems can improve that speed to 100–120 wpm. But automated speech recognition can handle speech at approximately 160 wpm. Pocket-sized computers have made speech recognition even more useful. A free iPhone app, such as Dragon Dictation, can record a brief sentence or a much longer composition. The speech is transformed into text that can be e-mailed, sent as a text message, or edited before transmitting to others to read.

The science of speech recognition is fairly amazing when one considers the irregularity of natural languages, such as English, further complicated by the acoustics of spoken language. No one ever says a given word exactly the same way twice. When words come at the beginning of a sentence or at the end of a sentence, they are pronounced differently. The length of time spent on a vowel

(continues on page 46)

00110101001010011101011010101010110010100001

The Rise and Fall of Shorthand

Shorthand is a system of abbreviation in which only a bare outline of a word is written—just enough to allow the user to later decipher from the symbol and its context what the word is. Shorthand systems go for maximum speed at the expense of readability. The process of writing in shorthand is called *stenography,* from the Greek *stenos* (narrow) and *graphē* or *graphie* (writing). A typical shorthand system provides symbols or abbreviations for words and common phrases, which can allow someone well trained in the system to write as quickly as people speak.

Shorthand was used more widely in the past, before the invention of recording and dictation machines. Until recently, shorthand was considered an essential part of secretarial training, as well as being useful for journalists. Although the primary use of shorthand has been to record oral dictation or discourse, some systems are still used for compact expression. For example, health care professionals may use shorthand notes in medical charts and correspondence. Shorthand notes are typically temporary, intended either for immediate use or later transcription.

The best-known shorthand systems include the Pitman system, developed

Most people speak at about 120 wpm (words per minute) but type only about 30 wpm. All but the fastest typists can only type around 100 wpm. Since most people can speak much more quickly than they can type, an individual could save much time in drafting documents if he or she could speak the words of the document to create the words on the page. Until recently, businesspeople achieved this result by dictating to a secretary or other transcriptionist, who would write down the spoken words and type them later. Now, many businesspeople either rely entirely on automatic speech recognition software to perform the same function or rely on human transcriptionists solely to make corrections to the transcripts produced by the software. (*Trinity Mirror/Mirrorpix/Alamy*)

00110101001010011101011010101010110010100001

Shorthand

Pitman		Gregg	Pitman		Gregg
—	K	⌒	(	TH	⌣
—	G	⌐	/	CH	/
⌒	M	—	/	I	/
⌣	N	—	)	Z	⟨
⌣	NG	＼		Z	⟨
＼	P	⌠	⌡	SH	′
＼	B	⌠	⌡	ZH	
|	T	⟋	♂	H	•
|	D	⟋	℘	H	
○	S	⟜	⟋	R	⌣
)	S	⟿	＼	R	
⌣	F	⟩	⌐	L	⌣
＼	V	⌡	⌡	W	⌢
(	TH	⌐	⌡	Y	⟠

© Infobase Learning

The process of dictation involves one person writing down the words spoken by another person while those words are being spoken so that the speech can later be typed into a document. Because it is not possible to write down speech by hand as quickly as it is spoken, various systems of shorthand were developed to enable secretaries and other transcriptionists to record dictated speech without falling behind the speaker. Shorthand systems are designed to make it possible to write words as quickly as possible. This table shows the symbols used by two prominent shorthand systems, known as the Pitman and Gregg systems.

in Britain by Sir Isaac Pitman in 1837. It is phonetically based, using geometrical curves and lines in varying lengths and angles. John Robert Gregg devised the most famous system in 1888. Gregg shorthand won out over Pitman shorthand in America and was widely taught in public schools as an essential skill needed

(continues)

001101010010100111010110101010101011001010000

(continued)

by office workers to take dictation. Gregg shorthand is based on outlines of words.

Various other systems of rapid writing based on alphabetic print or long-hand characters have been devised. Teeline, Speedwriting, Stenoscript, Forkner, Easyscript, AlphaHand, Baine's Typed Shorthand, HySpeed Longhand, Abbrevia-trix, Quickhand, and Carter Briefhand are examples. Keyscript, a system based on Pitman's, claims to be the fastest of the alphabetic systems. Most newer systems require few symbols to be learned, but rather consist of rules for abbreviating words together with memorized abbreviations. If the rules are consistently applied, they can be reversed to decode notes. These systems have the advantage of working with pen and paper and with keyboards.

Shorthand, of course, has not entirely disappeared. Students still create their own note-taking shortcuts, and journalists still supplement recordings with scribbled notes. And a new form of shorthand is probably present in most people's lives: The abbreviations and slang that make up text speak (or, to be brief, txtspk) may have originated through necessity, as people exchanged text messages on tiny mobile phone screens with even tinier keyboards. Phrases such as lol and omg have spread through the Internet into everyday conversation.

001101010010100111010110101010101011001010000

(continued from page 43)

is different when it is emphasized by the speaker. Consonants are pronounced differently depending upon the vowels that follows them. Furthermore, people do not pronounce words as distinct entities. For instance, "The stuff he knows can lead to problems" is acoustically identical to "The stuffy nose can lead to problems." English contains a vast number of homophones (words that sound the same but that may be spelled differently, such as *pair* and *pear* and *pare*). A computer program must not only grasp a complex language and take in all this acoustical information, but also evaluate the context and determine meaning.

No matter how advanced they become, automatic speech recognition systems still do not do everything that a skilled administrative assistant taking dictation can. For example, an assistant can:

- Take instructions about missing information ("Insert John Smith's mailing address here") and fill in details later
- Understand general instructions about content ("Close the letter by saying something nice about Mr. Smith's family and proposing that we get together the next time I am in Chicago; check my calendar so you can give him a specific date")
- Correct grammar and word-choice errors
- Refer to previously used text ("Insert that paragraph about insurance that we included in the letter I dictated to you this morning")

Automatic speech recognition and a human transcriptionist or editor can work well together to achieve many of the above benefits. For instance, a speaker could dictate a draft via automatic speech recognition software, and a human administrative assistant could review the draft, correct errors, and fill in details.

DOCUMENT ASSEMBLY

Document assembly software is used to create multiple versions of the same document; most of the document remains the same from version to version, but some of the content may change. The most familiar example of this process is the *mail merge* feature available in most word processing applications. When a user wants to send the same letter to multiple people, he or she first creates a skeleton document, or *template.* The template contains the *fixed text,* which will not vary from copy to copy—in this instance, the return address and the main body of the letter. The template must also include *fields,* which act as placeholders for the *variable text.* Each field is given a name. In a letter, examples of such fields are RecipientFirstName, RecipientLastName, StreetAddress, City, State, and ZipCode. The next step is to provide the document assembly system with the variable text. In the case of a letter, this might consist of a list of recipients and their mailing addresses, stored in a spreadsheet or word processing document. The document assembly system then takes over, creating a copy of the template and placing each unit of variable text into the template copy at the locations indicated by the placeholder fields. The document assembly system repeats this process for each unit of variable text, creating a separate copy of the document for each recipient.

More advanced document assembly systems have even more features. For example, they can adapt grammar or wording based on variable text. For example,

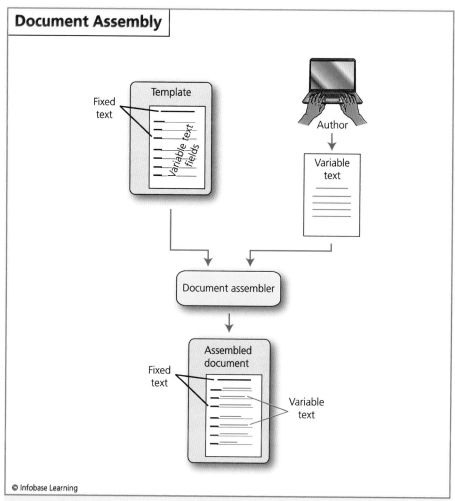

Document Assembly

Template

Fixed
text

Variable text
fields

Author

Variable
text

Document assembler

Assembled
document

Fixed
text

Variable
text

© Infobase Learning

Many individuals, businesses, government agencies, and other organizations need to send
letters and other documents to large numbers of people frequently. Often all copies of
the document are identical except for small amounts of content that vary based on the
person to whom the document is being sent. For example, when a telephone company
sends telephone bills each month, all of the bills are identical except for the listing of services and their corresponding prices. It would be highly inefficient for the telephone company's workers to retype all of the text in each bill manually. Instead, document assembly
software is used to automatically generate the bills using a template that includes both
fixed text (the text that is the same for all bills) and placeholder fields for variable text
(the text, such as prices, that varies). The document assembly software then generates a
bill for each customer by making a copy of the template and inserting personalized text
into the variable text fields. The text for the variable text fields may either be typed by a
human or copied automatically from a database.

if a letter is addressed to an individual, it might refer to "you" at various points in the letter. But if another letter is addressed to a company, the software can automatically substitute "your company" for "you." These applications can also make changes to the document based on rules. For example, if a recipient lives in California, the document management system might automatically include an additional paragraph about laws that apply only in that state. Automated document processing software, such as HotDocs, can also publish templates to the Web and automate Adobe portable document format (PDF) form templates.

Most letters people receive from companies, such as bank statements, utility bills, or magazine subscription reminders, are customized automatically using document assembly software. That is how companies and governments generate large volumes of letters quickly and easily. Online e-mail newsletter services, such as Constant Contact, are essentially document assembly services that specialize in customized e-mail newsletters rather than word processing documents.

The average administrative assistant's responsibility with respect to document assembly has evolved from being the person who personally types each document to being a manager and organizer of the document creation process. Armed with the tools contained in a personal computer, a single administrative assistant fills the roles that were once served by publications departments, graphic designers, mailroom workers, and clerks.

MEETING SCHEDULING

A detailed calendar serves as command central for most offices. An administrative assistant who once kept track of her boss's appointments on a paper schedule can now turn to the desktop computer and organize the week's schedule, set up meetings, and create a list of tasks with deadline reminders in moments.

Microsoft Outlook is the industry standard for scheduling and interoffice e-mail, but so many calendar applications and online scheduling tools exist that any business can come up with a solution to fit their office routines. A major benefit to using these tools is a significant reduction in the number of e-mails and telephone calls going back and forth to schedule a meeting. These tools can be linked directly to an employee's calendar so others can view their availability directly. One such service, TimeBridge, has a feature called Meet with Me, which allows TimeBridge users to provide their own personalized webpages that others can use to schedule meetings with them. For example, if Sally has a TimeBridge Meet with Me webpage, others can visit that webpage, view available time slots on Sally's calendar (without seeing private information about existing appointments on Sally's calendar), and request a meeting with Sally. The webpage then notifies Sally of the request appointment and, if Sally confirms the meeting, the appointment can be placed automatically on both Sally's calendar and the calendar of the person who requested the meeting.

Once an administrative assistant sets up a meeting, scheduling software offers a number of timesaving tools. For example, the meeting invitation can be sent automatically to all meeting invitees. When the invitees open the invitation, the meeting can be added to their calendars with a single click. The scheduling software will also automatically send meeting reminders to all attendees, as far in advance as they would like. Some software even has a snooze feature that can be set to remind invitees again in a few days, hours, or minutes. In this era of global communications, a meeting can be tied in to a conference call number or online meeting room so people around the world can participate through phone and video connections, many of which are available at low cost or even for free.

If a business uses these tools, the role of the administrative assistant in meeting planning shifts to one of sending out invitations, scheduling meeting rooms, preparing materials, and arranging for other accommodations, rather than coordinating schedules directly. However, even some of these functions, such as requesting audiovisual equipment, are increasingly being automated.

TRAVEL PLANNING

Once, planning a trip meant that an administrative assistant would call the airport or the train station or even visit the ticket desks in person to make arrangements. Or perhaps a business would work with a travel agent who would enter all the relevant information on a green monochrome computer screen. Travel agents were the keepers of all travel information, and consumers never made their own arrangements. Then the Internet era dawned. Travel information became available directly to consumers, and travel plans could be made all in one place through online services such as Expedia and Travelocity, along with many others. Many administrative assistants handle arrangements through commercial sites or through a corporate travel system that handles travel authorization, reservations, and expense tracking.

Frank Levy and Richard J. Murnane, Authors of *The New Division of Labor: How Computers Are Creating the Next Job Market*

In their book *The New Division of Labor: How Computers Are Creating the Next Job Market,* Richard Murnane, professor at the Harvard Graduate School of Education, and Frank Levy, professor of urban economics at MIT, write that the future belongs to people who excel at problem-solving and complex communication—that is, interacting with others to acquire information, understand that information, and persuade others of its implications.

Richard Murnane, economist and professor of education and society at Harvard, who studies how computer technology affects the demands for skills in the U.S. economy *(Tom Kates)*

The book, the second they have written together, tells stories of people at work—a high-end financial adviser, a customer service representative, a pair of successful chefs, a cardiologist, an auto mechanic, the author Victor Hugo, and floor traders in a London financial exchange. The authors merge these stories with insights from cognitive science, computer science, and economics to show how computers are enhancing productivity in many jobs even as they eliminate others—both directly and by sending work overseas. At greatest risk are jobs that can be expressed in programmable rules—blue collar, clerical, and similar work that requires moderate skills and used to pay middle class wages. The loss of these jobs leaves a growing division between those who can and cannot earn a good living in the computerized economy.

(continues)

001101010010100111010110101010101011001010000 1

(continued)

The coauthors argue that advances in technology, rather than reducing America's workforce, have actually restructured job distribution: "The challenge now is to provide our high-school graduates with the skills they will need to gain access to the growing number of technical, professional, and managerial jobs," Murnane asserts. "Many of those jobs now require some level of higher education or special training, and our students have to be prepared to take advantage of those opportunities."

They urge educators to help students develop complex communication and expert thinking skills. For instance, today's customer service representatives not only must use databases competently, draft e-mails, and manage automated telephone services and webpages, but also must know how to respond to unexpected customer concerns. Workers unskilled in the art of complex communication—observing, listening, persuading, and negotiating—will simply be less sought after in the Internet age.

Similarly, as machines take over many basic, repetitive tasks that humans used to perform, workers increasingly require more training to use new technology effectively. For example, good auto mechanics need to know what to do next when the computer diagnostics say that a car has no problem, yet the car still does not operate properly. If high schools neglect to teach students how to think expertly—to apply learned knowledge from one set of circumstances to new, open-ended situations—the authors warn that graduates will be unprepared for the growing number of jobs that provide a middle class salary in an economy increasingly populated by machines.

In a 1997 *Newshour* interview with David Gergen, editor at large of *U.S. News & World Report,* the two economists elaborated on what they call "the new basic

001101010010100111010110101010101011001010000 1

The features available on travel sites have expanded greatly: in one visit, a trip planner can take care of hotel, airfare, and car rental for multiple destinations. Event and sightseeing tickets can be purchased at the same time, as can travel insurance. Reviews from other travelers are available, which might warn of construction work or shoddy housekeeping in a hotel. These systems can also store personal profiles with information, such as preferred time of travel, airline seat choice, and frequent skills." To qualify for a job that will pay a middle class wage, they said, a graduate needs to be able to read well enough to understand training manuals, do the mathematics typically included in training manuals, solve problems, communicate effectively orally and in writing, work productively with people from different backgrounds, and have enough familiarity with computers to learn to use new software.

Frank Levy joined the faculty at MIT in 1992 and previously taught for 10 years each at the University of California, Berkeley, and the University of Maryland, College Park. He has also been a senior research associate at the Urban Institute. He received his bachelor's degree in economics from MIT in 1963 and his doctorate in economics from Yale in 1969. Levy's recent research has focused on the ways computer technology is reshaping the labor market. He has also done research on income inequality and living standards in the United States and the economics of education.

Richard Murnane is Thompson Professor of Education and Society at the Harvard Graduate School of Education and a research associate at the National Bureau of Economic Research. He has examined how computer-based technological change has affected skill demands in the U.S. economy and the consequences of initiatives designed to improve public education—for example, the practice of providing salary bonuses to attract skilled teachers to high-need schools. Murnane is codirector of a large research project examining the ways that increased earnings inequality in the United States affects opportunities for children from low-income families to obtain a good education. He earned a bachelor's degree in economics from Williams College in 1966 and a doctorate from Yale University in 1974. In addition to teaching at Yale and other universities, he spent three years teaching high school mathematics in Houston, Baltimore, and Washington, D.C.

traveler program credits. Travel sites, such as Fodor's and Lonely Planet, provide online travel guides for those making trips to distant destinations, and products like schmap.com allow users to download a bit of software that updates regularly with the latest information on good places to eat, drink, and see in a range of destinations.

Travel planning is often tied to the task of meeting and conference planning. Conferences have changed greatly through digital technology and the Internet.

Not long ago, presentations were a lot more like lectures, perhaps with the added feature of a presenter who droned his way through a set of PowerPoint slides. Now social media have entered the picture, bringing online tools such as webinars. More than ever, the administrative assistant must be a multitasker. There are so many new ways to gain information, book a venue, send invitations, and promote an event. Organizers have multiple tools at their disposal to keep in contact with meeting participants, such as e-mail updates, online surveys, and more.

CONCLUSIONS

Every executive, manager, and other supervisor who has employed an administrative assistant knows that they are critical not only to the success of the business but to the executive's personal success. Although some view the job of an administrative assistant as a relatively low-level or unskilled job, nothing could be farther from the truth, particularly in the Internet age. Today's administrative assistant must not only be conversant with a wide variety of technologies but also be capable of learning how to adapt to new technologies rapidly and competently. Many administrative assistants find themselves training their bosses to use new technologies and keeping others in the company up-to-date on the latest technological developments. Companies now often seek the input and advice of administrative assistants on how to improve the administrative operations of the company.

Such changes are reflected in the changing nature of the terms that are used to refer to administrative assistants. Although at first the job title "secretary" was most common, titles such as "administrative assistant" and "executive assistant" came into more frequent use to reflect the wider variety of skills and responsibilities associated with the job. Many people who started their careers as administrative assistants now find themselves as office managers and in other roles that subsume the responsibilities that previously would have been divided among several employees in several departments. Although such increased responsibility can carry with it additional stress, it can also make the job particularly satisfying, especially for those who enjoy using and learning about new technologies every day.

4

MANAGERS: BUSINESS INFORMATION AT YOUR FINGERTIPS

Keeping track of employees, projects, finances, and sales is essential to a business's profitability. Some small businesses rely still on traditional methods, such as typewriters and filing cabinets, to manage business information and processes, but every sizable business uses computer hardware, software, and networks to automate and manage at least some of its operations. Technology helps businesses to perform existing processes more efficiently and reliably and to track information and provide products and services in ways that were not possible before the advent of computers.

BUDGETING AND ACCOUNTING

Accounting professionals now typically use computer software to keep books and manage budgets, in place of the paper ledger books that dominated accounting until the late 20th century. One of the most popular accounting software packages is QuickBooks, which offers the digital equivalent of a paper checking register in which checks and other expenses can be recorded. Entering a check in a bank account register in QuickBooks causes the balance of the bank account to be updated automatically, and the account can then be reconciled automatically against a statement issued by the bank at the end of the month and downloaded directly into the software, eliminating hours of manual cross-referencing of the business's records against the bank's records. Businesses that need the extra functionality of an enterprise-level accounting application, with features that enable large accounting departments to share data and generate complex reports, can choose from software such as QuickBooks Enterprise Solutions and Sage Peachtree Accounting. Most enterprise accounting applications support advanced features such as payroll management, budget forecasting, inventory, banking, billing, job tracking, general ledger, asset management, invoicing, and shipment tracking. Such software can be used to automatically comply with legal requirements, such as the creation of reports required by securities law (e.g., 10-K and 10-Q reports that corporations must file with the Securities and Exchange Commission [SEC]).

Creating budget forecasts is an example of a process that is very time consuming to perform manually. For example, predicting the total value of a company's assets at the end of the next fiscal year requires taking into account the company's current assets, previous revenue and expenses, current trends in revenue and expenses, and potential future changes in revenue and expenses. This can be particularly difficult to do in a large company in which such information is spread throughout many divisions. This is one area in which modern accounting software saves a particularly significant amount of time because it can perform all of the necessary calculations essentially instantaneously. Furthermore, if all of a company's financial information is stored in its computers and such computers are networked, the company's financial software can make highly accurate forecasts because it can draw directly on current information from throughout the company instead of relying on old information or current estimates.

Accounting software is also particularly useful for considering the potential financial impact of future changes in circumstances. Most accounting software enables the user to view the impact of so-called what-if scenarios, such as changes in revenue, expenses, number of sales, interest rates, and currency exchange rates on the company's profits, assets, and liabilities. For example, a company can view the predicted impact of a 5 percent decline in revenues on the ability of the company to make its debt payments on time, the impact of a 5 percent increase in revenues on the company's ability to hire more employees, or the impact of a 0.5 percent increase in interest rates on the company's profits. Before the development of accounting software, such predictions were much more an art than a science and could only very roughly estimate the effects of future events on the company's financial health.

PROJECT MANAGEMENT

Project management software is used to plan for and execute projects involving multiple people and many resources over time. Examples of such projects include constructing an office building, designing a new cell phone, organizing a conference, and moving a company from one city to another.

Such projects can be very difficult to manage because they involve so many different factors that interrelate in complex ways. For example, assembling a panel of speakers at a conference may require negotiating fees with those speakers, making travel arrangements for them, reserving a room, and advertising for the event, all on a fixed budget. If one speaker requires a higher fee than expected, this reduces the amount of funds available for travel and advertising. If a famous speaker agrees to participate, this may draw a larger crowd, requiring a larger and more expensive room, but also generate higher revenue in the form of increased ticket sales. It can be difficult or impossible to keep track of the interrelationships among all of these aspects of a project manually, particularly if elements of the project change quickly and repeatedly over time, and if many elements of the project depend on each other according to complicated relationships. The fear of every project manager is that a small change in one aspect of a project—such as the inability to secure an advertisement for a conference in a newspaper by a particular date—will have unexpected ripple effects throughout the project that will cause the entire endeavor to fail. Project management software can help those who manage projects to predict which actions will need to be taken, by which employees, when, and at what cost, even as circumstances change.

Some of the questions that project management software can answer for project managers include:

- How many people will be needed to work on a particular project and what skills will they need to have?
- If a deadline in the project is missed, what impact will that have on the ability to complete the entire project on time?
- If one member of the project team leaves the project or becomes sick, what skills must that person's replacement have to ensure that the project stays on track?
- If the project must be completed sooner than originally planned, will it be less expensive to require the existing project team members to

work longer hours until the project is complete or to hire additional team members?

- If a new requirement is added to the project (e.g., a new feature that needs to be included in a cell phone), what impact will that have on the cost of the project, on its completion date, and on the number of people required?

In recent years, the concept of project management has evolved into the concepts of *business process automation* and *business process modeling.* Business process automation is the computer age equivalent of printed office *operations manuals* that employees would follow to carry out common office tasks. For

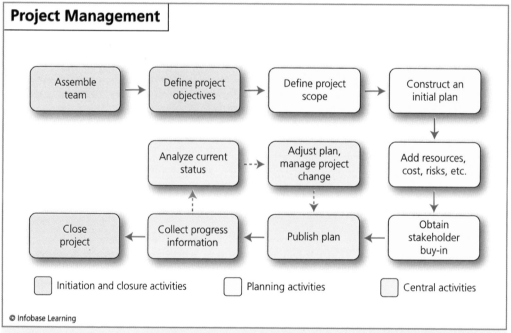

Project Management

Managing and executing a large project, such as designing a new automobile, planning a conference, or moving a business from one office to another, requires organizing a team of people with diverse skills, acquiring the funds and materials necessary to perform the project, and coordinating the activities of all team members so that they can accomplish their tasks as efficiently as possible. Modern businesses use project management software to facilitate managing such projects. For example, if one member of the project team fails to meet a deadline, the project management software can automatically calculate the impact of such a failure on the ability of other team members to meet their deadlines. This diagram shows one model of project management which can either be performed manually or partially automated using project management software.

example, most companies have written procedures that describe what needs to be done when a new employee is hired. Such a procedure might include, for example, assigning a mailbox and phone number to the new employee, providing the employee with an office, establishing a benefits package for the employee, adding the employee to the payroll, providing an initial training session to the employee, and so on. These procedures require the participation and cooperation of multiple people across multiple departments, such as human resources, accounting, and physical plant. Traditionally, all of these steps were written on a piece of paper to be carried out manually and coordinated by an office manager. This can become quite complex and time consuming, particularly when the initiation of one task relies on the completion of other tasks. For example, it might not be possible to provide someone with an e-mail address until that person's contact information has been added into the company's employee list.

Business process automation software attempts to automate these processes so that as many individual steps as possible can be performed automatically. Ideally, no employee needs to be responsible for managing the process. Instead, the company might program in the logic of the new employee setup procedure, and then all that the company needs to do upon hiring a new employee is to click a button. In response, the business process automation software provides instructions to all of the relevant employees to let them know what they need to do as part of the process. As each person involved in the process completes a task, he or she marks that task as complete in the business process automation software. In response, subsequent tasks are automatically triggered and assigned to the correct people. Because this software manages the flow of work among multiple people, it is sometimes called *workflow automation software.*

SUPPLY CHAIN MANAGEMENT

A *supply chain* is a system of people, products, and resources used to create and distribute products efficiently. For example, when a consumer purchases a bottle of water for $1, the actual profit is only a few pennies. The supply chain for creating a bottle of water includes the workers at a bottling factory, machines to create the bottles, apply the labels, and fill the bottles with water, quality control specialists, lightbulbs and toilet paper for the company offices, accountants, lawyers, and the costs of distribution. Making these processes more efficient can save

(continues on page 62)

The Paperless Office

A *paperless office* is a workplace at which the use of paper has been completely eliminated. The benefits of a paperless office are obvious: it saves trees, makes copying or sharing documents easier, reduces costs, and saves space.

The idea of a paperless office was first introduced in 1975 as a technological buzzword. It was not considered a real possibility by most experts due to technological limitations of the day and the universal reliance on paper. Companies such as Xerox and IBM worked toward developing technologies that could make certain aspects of an office paperless, such as electronic word processors, but a completely paperless office remained out of reach. In the original conception of a paperless office, a personal computer would eliminate most routine tasks, such as keeping records and filing. As computers became more powerful, however, photocopiers and printers also increased in power and decreased in price. As a result, the increased use of computers actually led to increased use of paper, as computer users developed a habit of printing drafts of long documents just to review them once and then recycle them. Similarly, a company might distribute thousands of copies of a single memo on paper to all of its employees rather than post a single copy on a bulletin board in the break room simply because printing copies had become so easy and inexpensive.

Early adoption of paperless systems was further limited by the poor resolution of computer monitors. Reading long documents on early screens was uncomfortable, so users opted to print the documents instead, negating the purpose of storing documents electronically in the first place. It was also difficult to share documents internally; networks were not as powerful as they are now, so the quickest way to move a document from computer to computer was to put it on a floppy disk. This was still slower than its paper counterpart. Paper documents could also be tossed in a briefcase and carried to a meeting; a desktop computer was not mobile, and even laptop computers could weigh 10 pounds or more until recently.

A modern paperless office, implemented correctly, avoids many of the problems with the early paperless office. Electronic documents are now easily storable and transmissible across widely available computer networks, and screens

1100111010010101010100110010111011010100101001

For most of the 20th century, offices were populated by workers sitting at desks, reading books, writing on paper pads, and surrounded by paper files. File rooms contained rows of file cabinets containing all of the organization's critical information, and human file clerks were responsible for creating, organizing, updating, and retrieving such files. With the move toward paperless offices, physical files are becoming a thing of the past. Instead, office workers increasingly can access, edit, and share all of the information they need solely using computers. As a result, the desk cluttered with paper may soon exist only in history books. *(Dimitriy Shironosov/Shutterstock, Inc.)*

on e-book readers and other devices have become nearly as easy on the eyes as paper. Yet the paperless office continues to face challenges. Digital recording media, such as tapes, floppy diskettes, hard disks, CDs, and flash drives, tend to become obsolete quickly. As a result, maintaining a paperless office over an extended period of time can require dedicating a significant number of person-hours every few years to convert data from old archival formats to a newer formats. Electronic documents present aesthetic problems as well, such as the difficulty of viewing electronic documents side by side, highlighting text, and marking up content quickly.

(continues)

1100111010010101010100110010111011010100101001

(continued)

Nonetheless, many modern companies have insisted on going paperless or at least "paper-less" by reducing their use of paper very significantly even if not entirely. The prevalence of high-speed, always-on wired and wireless Internet connections has significantly improved the performance of networks. Large, high-quality monitor configurations create less eyestrain while reading on a computer. Highly mobile laptops and cloud-based file storage have made it possible to view documents on any computer from anywhere. In general, the benefits of enabling employees to view, edit, and share only a single electronic copy of each document from any location at any time increasingly outweigh any remaining drawbacks of electronic documents in comparison to their paper counterparts.

(continued from page 59)

consumers money. Modern *supply chain management* involves using software packages to manage design, planning, execution, monitoring, and control of all of these infrastructure elements within a business. Supply chain management addresses issues such as how many distributors a manufacturer should use, where those distributors should be located, which distribution strategy costs the least, and the quantity and location of raw materials and finished goods.

The concept of supply chain management goes back to the Ford assembly line. Since market forces are constantly changing the supply and demand for products, even experts at managing supplies would often simply guess at the kind and number of parts that should be at any particular factory or distributor at any particular point in time. The problem with such guesses is that providing too many parts to a particular location would result in some of them going unused, thereby resulting in a waste of company assets, while providing too few parts (or the wrong kinds of parts) to a particular location would result in the company's inability to produce as many products as it could sell, thereby reducing the company's profits. As commerce entered the era of globalization, supply chain management became a critical factor for nearly every major corporation, and software packages were developed as early as the 1980s to begin to address this problem.

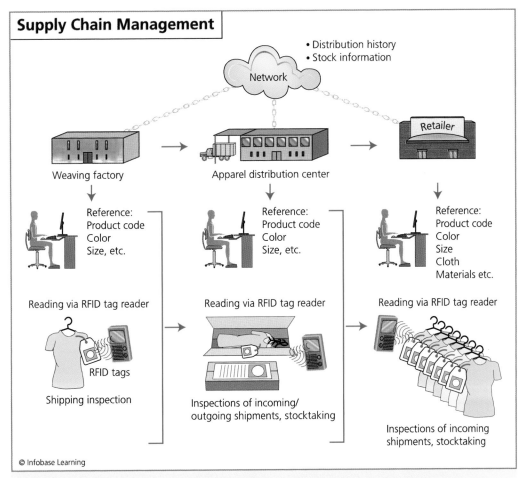

A supply chain is a collection of people, technologies, processes, and resources involved in creating a product and transporting it from its suppliers to its customers. For example, in the case of a box of cereal, the supply chain begins with the farms that grow and harvest the grain, through the trucking companies that transport the grain to the cereal manufacturer, from the cereal manufacturer to its wholesale distributors, from the wholesale distributors to the supermarket, and from the supermarket to the consumer who buys the cereal. Managing a supply chain can be complex because the failure of any supplier to perform its services can cause the rest of the chain to grind to a halt. As a result, large companies use formal supply chain management procedures to ensure that their products can be manufactured and sold despite any problems that arise. Supply chain management software can help not only to automate supply chain management but to identify changed circumstances (such as a decrease in the price of grain or dry weather) that might have an impact on the supply chain in the future, so the company can take proactive steps to ensure continued smooth functioning.

Although each business has a unique supply chain, two concepts of supply chain management apply to all supply chains and have revolutionized business. First, *just-in-time distribution* allows companies to create products after orders for those products have been placed. Companies that use just-in-time distribution prepare a ledger of all the purchases made every day and then instruct their distributors to fill these orders "just in time" for shipping to the retailer or customer. The benefits of a just-in-time supply chain include reduced inventory costs (because the company does not need to maintain a large inventory of products in its warehouses in anticipation of receiving orders for them in the future) and a flexible and scalable distribution center. For example, when Dell began using the *direct model* supply chain management strategy to sell PCs directly to end-users, they were able to sell computers far less expensively than their competitors, providing a large margin of cost-savings to users, and thereby increasing Dell's market share. Bypassing distributors and retailers allows Dell to properly identify market segments, analyze the requirements of each segment, and develop accurate forward-looking demand forecasts and adapt their supply chain accordingly.

MARKETING AND SALES

Computers and the Internet are now used extensively for marketing and sales. According to the Internet Advertising Bureau, $24 billion is spent every year on Internet advertising. Internet commerce results in $133.7 billion of sales per year. Advertising is the primary source of revenue for industry giants such as Google, and a significant secondary source of revenue for Web-based companies such as Amazon.

The earliest Internet advertisements were *banner advertisements*—rectangular advertisements placed on the top, bottom, or sides of webpages in fixed locations to attract the reader's attention, much like advertisements placed in newspapers and magazines. A more recent form of advertising is *contextual advertising,* which identifies the topic of a page by scanning it for keywords and then placing advertisements related to that topic on the page. This was pioneered by Google as part of its AdSense program. For example, if a Web site owner signs up to participate in the AdSense program, if the Web site contains an article about tennis, Google will automatically place advertisements for tennis-related products along the side of the page. If someone viewing the page clicks on one of the advertisements, the Web site owner receives a small payment as a commission.

Banner advertisements account for only 23 percent of total Internet advertisement spending today. *Search advertisements*—sponsored placement advertisements on search engine result pages—contribute to half of all Internet advertisement spending. *Rich media advertisements,* such as streaming video or interactive Flash ads that are displayed over or within the content of webpages, rather than beside them, have started to receive widespread adoption as Web site visitors have begun to grow immune to text-only ads, because ads containing audio and video are more likely to catch the user's attention.

Advertisers are not flying blind. Some, like DoubleClick, display ads to a particular user that are relevant to that user based on the user's browsing history. For example, if the user has been browsing the Amazon site, looking at hammocks, DoubleClick will likely display an ad for a hammock from one of Amazon's competitors in the webpage currently being viewed by the user. This type of targeted advertising uses what is called *behavioral tracking.* Other advertising networks, notably Facebook, use *demographic ad targeting.* For example, every Facebook user has provided certain demographic data—such as age, gender, and interests—that Facebook's advertisers use to select ads to display to those users that are intended to match the users' interests. For example, if a user lists "tennis" as an interest, Facebook will display advertisements to that user from local tennis coaches and tennis equipment stores.

Retailers such as Amazon provide *affiliate programs,* which allow Internet marketers to attract potential Amazon customers to their Web sites to benefit by redirecting those people to Amazon's product listings through targeted advertising. For example, a Web site dedicated to sporting goods might display advertisements for sports equipment available at Amazon. When a user clicks on that ad, the user is taken to the product listing at Amazon, and in exchange Amazon pays the originating Web site (Amazon's *affiliate*) between 4 and 10 percent if the user purchases the product from Amazon. For high-value items and low-volume items that sell in large quantities, this can be economically beneficial for everyone involved, including the retailer, who is happy to sell more products, the Internet marketer, who receives a profit for displaying the advertisement, and the advertiser, who receives a commission paid by the retailer.

Other techniques used by Internet marketers include *search engine optimization (SEO),* which refers to writing articles and otherwise tailoring the content of webpages with the intent of causing those them to obtain higher ranks in the search results produced by Google and other Internet search engines. Such high rankings are highly desired by owners of Web sites because most people who perform an Internet search only follow links that are at or near the top of the search result list. Although no one except the engineers at Google know exactly how Google's algorithm for ranking search results works, many SEO specialists have developed a good enough understanding of how to modify the contents of a webpage to cause it to place higher in search engine results to produce good track records of consistently obtaining high rankings for the Web sites they maintain on Google and elsewhere. Some factors that influence search result rankings are linking to other sites with those sites reciprocating the links and updating content frequently based on phrases that are commonly typed into search engines.

Customer Relationship Management

Customer relationship management (CRM) is the process of managing the relationship between a company and its customers. In the days before computers, CRM was a task handled solely by human account representatives and, in the case of the local mom-and-pop store, the individual owners of the business through their personal, day-to-day interactions with customers. Today, most large companies, particularly those that perform a significant amount of business over the Internet, use CRM software to manage and automate many aspects of their relationships with their customers. For example, modern CRM systems send out newsletters, welcome messages, and product promotion announcements, with the intent of turning visitors into customers, of keeping existing customers happy, and of generating as much revenue as possible for the business.

CRM software has become extremely powerful, in part because it can leverage large volumes of real-time data about the browsing and purchasing histories of individual customers to make decisions about how to interact with those customers. For example, CRM software might track how frequently individual customers respond favorably to marketing e-mails and then continue to send frequent marketing e-mails to those customers who respond to them by making purchases, while instead sending e-mails to infrequent responders asking if there is anything the company could do to increase the customers' satisfaction with the company. CRM software can also recommend specific products to

The growth of social networking has created new ways for Internet marketers to reach customers. Social media specialists primarily target ads at Twitter and Facebook users with the goal of *going viral*—spreading rapidly through sharing, commenting, and linking between friends. Viral marketing relies on the Kevin Bacon principle, also known as the principle of six degrees of separation, which is the premise that every person on Earth is connected to anyone else on Earth (including Kevin Bacon) by an average of six intermediary links (where a link is any connection between two people who know each other). If a meme goes viral, it will be seen by tens of millions within 24 hours.

a customer based on that customer's purchasing history and the purchasing history of other customers who have bought similar products. Such functions would be extremely tedious and time consuming to perform manually for each of the company's customers, due to the large amount of data that would need to be analyzed.

The most widely used CRM software is Salesforce. Salesforce's primary offering is its sales process automation service called the Sales Cloud. It is used by companies to handle all aspects of the sales process. It can track all of the company's leads (potential new customers), automatically generate e-mails to those leads, qualify the leads (determine how likely the leads are to be high-quality customers for the company), and generate reports of where in the process the company is with respect to each lead. The purpose is to help companies find, attract, and obtain new customers at a fraction of the cost of hiring a full-time, full-scale human sales force to perform all of the necessary steps manually. Although companies that use Salesforce must still have a human sales force, it can be smaller in number and less highly skilled than if no software were used to facilitate the sales process. The most innovative aspect of Salesforce when it was first launched was that it was provided solely through the Web as a kind of *software as a service (SaaS),* so that companies could use Salesforce without having to install any software on their own computers. As a result, Salesforce was one of the first prominent *application service providers (ASPs).* Now, SaaS and ASPs have become very prominent and widespread for a wide variety of services.

HUMAN RESOURCES

The human resources (HR) department of any organization is in charge of placing people into job openings and ensuring that they perform their jobs

William Henry Leffingwell, Early Proponent of Applying Scientific Management to Office Workers

William H. Leffingwell (1876–1934) was an efficiency expert who applied scientific management principles to office workers, such as typists and clerks, in much the same way that Frederick Taylor had applied scientific management to manual laborers. Before Leffingwell, most managers and economists assumed that scientific management was only applicable to so-called unskilled jobs such as those of mechanics, construction workers, and assembly line operators. Leffingwell, however, demonstrated that many of the same techniques could be applied to workers who we would today refer to as *knowledge workers*—those whose primary job tasks involve creating, revising, analyzing, and distributing information.

For example, Leffingwell proposed that there was one correct way to insert paper into a typewriter, one correct way to sit at one's desk, and one correct way to staple pages together. Leffingwell followed secretaries around as they did their daily work, sat behind typists and timed how many minutes they typed every day, and awarded bonuses to the workers who performed their tasks most efficiently. Leffingwell, the son of a woodworker and originally trained as a stenographer, was driven by the belief that workers were inherently lazy, seeking to avoid work whenever possible, and that as a result they needed to be instructed strictly and watched closely at all times.

Leffingwell's most lasting contributions are the books that he wrote on scientific management in the office, such as *Office Management: Principles and Practice, Textbook of Office Management,* and *Better Office Management,* in which he described in detail how he had adapted the techniques originally developed by Taylor and Ford to clerks, messengers, and typists. He believed that the same basic principles could be applied more generally to workers in service industries such as banking, accounting, and insurance. Although little is remembered or written about Leffingwell today, his work left a lasting impression on management theories and corporate executives. Any doctor, nurse, or hospital worker who today is required by an insurance company to use a computer to record every action he or successfully. The HR department of an organization handles hiring, firing, employee disputes, and oversight of the workforce. Before the widespread use of computers, HR departments found new candidates primarily through

she performs and the amount of time it took to complete that action has Leffingwell to thank—or to blame, depending on one's perspective—for the myriad procedures that now govern every aspect of the operation of a modern medical facility.

Most managers of corporations in the 20th century believed that workers would work most efficiently if rigid structures, such as formal dress codes, strict work hours, and uniform work spaces, were imposed on them. This photograph shows a typical office setting in 1948. Pioneers in the personal computer industry and other high-tech industries adopted a more relaxed style in the late 20th and early 21st centuries, in which dress codes were significantly loosened and employees had significant freedom to decorate their work spaces and even to set their own work hours. The successes of the computer industry have influenced corporations in many other industries to adopt some of the same practices, partially in response to demands from workers and partially in an effort to cultivate innovation and creativity. *(Charles Babbage Institute; Burroughs/Unisys Archives, University of Minnesota, Minneapolis)*

advertisements in newspapers or magazines, employment agencies, and personal referrals.

Today, many more job openings can be found on any of several job search Web sites, including Monster, Career Builder, LinkedIn, TheLadders, and One-Wire. Each of these networks provides a slightly different job search market for different clientele. TheLadders, for instance, only posts jobs starting above $100,000 a year. Monster and Career Builder, by comparison, feature more jobs at the lower end of the spectrum, including internships, entry level, and trade skill employment. LinkedIn can inform members of job opportunities that are relevant to them based on information in their LinkedIn profiles, such as their skills, experience, and current job title.

Accepting résumés from Internet users seems like a step forward for HR specialists. The drawbacks associated with posting job information online include more applications from unqualified users, risk of identity theft, and the inability to chat face-to-face if the applicant is from another area of the country.

CONCLUSIONS

Modern businesses would grind to a halt without computers and the Internet. Even the seemingly simple task of sending out detailed and customized bills to all of the customers of a telephone, cable television, or electricity utility company every month would be impossible to perform in a cost-efficient manner without electronic databases for storing the billing information for each customer and for generating the bills themselves. That is because as a business grows in size, the cost and complexity of maintaining its records and running its internal operations can grow exponentially. The simple systems that suffice for a small company, such as index cards for storing the addresses of customers or window signs for advertising sales, are inadequate for the needs of a larger company. Furthermore, internal communications among a company's employees grow more complex as the company grows. Only with the use of computer technology can businesses continue to manage such complexity as they grow without their costs skyrocketing. It is not unreasonable to conclude that computers and electronic communication technology are as responsible for the growth of large-scale modern corporations as improvements in transportation, manufacturing, and agriculture.

Businesses strive to increase the efficiency of their operations—such as by increasing the number of products they can manufacture per dollar invested or per person-hour worked—because increases in efficiency result in increased profits, at least in the short term. Imagine that it costs a shoe manufacturer $10 to make a pair of shoes and that the manufacturer sells that pair of shoes to its wholesalers for $15. This represents a profit of $5 per pair, or a profit margin of approximately 33 percent: ($15 − $10)/$15 ≈ 0.33 ≈ 33 percent. If the manufacturer can increase the efficiency with which it manufacturers those shoes so that it only costs the company $7.50 instead of $10 to make each pair, and the company can still sell each pair to its wholesalers for $15, then the manufacturer has increased its profit margin to 50 percent: ($15 − $7.50) / $15 = 0.50 = 50 percent.

As this simple example shows, companies are always seeking to drive down their costs because doing so increases their profits. This increase, however, is only temporary. Over time, as other manufacturers discover how to reduce the amount they need to spend to make a pair of shoes, they too will obtain increased profits. Eventually, however, one company will likely attempt to sell a larger number of shoes than its competitors by reducing the price at which it sells each pair of shoes to its wholesalers. As that company's sales increase, the other shoe manufacturers will begin to reduce their prices as well, in what is known as a price war. The end result—lower-priced products—is good for consumers and is one of the most beneficial effects of competition in a market economy.

At the end of this cycle, however, all of the companies in the shoe manufacturing business are likely to stand on relatively equal footing. As a result, they will all have an incentive to once again seek ways to increase the efficiencies of the operations to obtain competitive advantages over each other. In this way, the market continuously drives improvements in efficiency that lower prices for consumers.

This book and the five others in the Computers, Internet, and Society set describe how computers and the Internet can help increase efficiency in a variety of ways, such as by using project management software to enable products to be designed more quickly, by eliminating the use of paper so that employees can create and share information effortlessly and less expensively, by managing a company's supply chain so that raw materials are always purchased at the lowest possible price and are available when needed, and by finding the most competent employees to hire from among large numbers of candidates. These benefits are compounded by the fact that the price of computer hardware and software itself continues to drop as its power increases. As a result, businesses will likely continue to increasingly rely on digital technology to enable them to drive down costs, run their internal operations more smoothly, and keep their customers happy, all in an effort to keep their profit margins as high as possible for as long as possible—until their competitors catch up and they need to return once again to the drawing board.

5

COMPUTER PROGRAMMERS: CREATING SOFTWARE FOR CREATING SOFTWARE

Computer programmers are in a unique position with respect to the impact of computers on their jobs. Most workers do their jobs using whatever tools their employers make available to them. In fact, many employers prohibit their employees from bringing their own tools to use on the job and from using tools for particular tasks other than the ones that the employer has instructed them to use. Furthermore, most employees are only trained in using tools, not in designing them, and therefore most employees could not create new tools for use in their own jobs even if they wanted and were allowed by their employers to do so.

In contrast, computer programmers both have the skill to create new software and are specifically hired to do so. Even if a programmer is hired only to write the code for a Web browser, if the programmer, as part of her job, creates software that can measure the speed of the Web browser automatically, such software can be used by that programmer and other programmers to design the Web browser more efficiently and to create a better end product. Many employers of programmers, therefore, not only allow but encourage programmers to create new software that helps them to do their jobs. As a result, programmers often design software that can automate or otherwise facilitate the performance of aspects of their own jobs.

This chapter explores some of the ways in which computer programmers and engineers have continuously improved computer technology in ways that have repeatedly redefined the work performed by computer professionals.

HARDWIRING EARLY SOFTWARE

Today, the term *software* is often used interchangeably with code. Software is created by writing instructions in the form of *source code,* which are then translated into *object code.* (See the following section, "Compilers," for more details on source code and object code.) Software is viewed as a kind of information, an intangible substance that can be stored and transmitted in the form of electrical and magnetic signals but not held in one's hand like a toaster or a radio.

This was not always true. Software was once quite hard. For example, in 1801, the French inventor Joseph-Marie Jacquard (1752–1834) invented a loom that has been known ever since as the *Jacquard loom.* Before the Jacquard loom, loom operators would use manual looms to weave patterns into cloth. The Jacquard loom largely automated this process by enabling patterns to be encoded onto *punched cards.* These were cards in which holes were punched in an arrangement that corresponded to the desired pattern. A human operator would feed the cards into the loom, which would weave the specified pattern into cloth automatically. Changing the pattern on the cards would cause the loom to weave another design. A particular stack of punched cards with a specific pattern of holes on it therefore was a kind of software for the loom, because it represented a set of instructions to the loom for creating a particular cloth pattern. The example of the Jacquard loom, in which software was stored on paper rather than in an electronic memory, demonstrates that software need not take the form of electrical or magnetic signals. The Jacquard loom was a commercial success; in France alone 11,000 Jacquard looms were in use by 1812.

Punched cards continued to play a significant role in programmable machines well into the 20th century. Machines based on punched cards received a boost in popularity when the U.S. Census Office selected such a machine, invented by Herman Hollerith (whose company later merged with two others to form IBM), to tabulate the results of the 1890 census. The Census Office had held a public contest for a more efficient way to count and interpret census results after it took seven years to tally the results of the 1880 census, leading the office to realize that it would be impossible to count the results of the 1890 census by the turn of the century without a faster system. Hollerith won the contract by demonstrating that his machine could count results more than twice as quickly as either of its competitors. His machines encoded census data about a particular individual—such as his or her race, sex, and nationality—on a punched card.

According to *Electrical Engineer* in 1891, the Hollerith tabulator "works unerringly as the mills of the gods, but beats them hollow as to speed."

Although the punched cards in early machines were used solely to store data, such as the answers to census questions, eventually machines were developed for which punched cards could store programs—sequences of instructions to control the actions of the machines. For example, the Harvard Mark I computer, completed in 1944 by Howard Aiken, could process programs and data provided to it on punched paper tape, punched cards, or dial switches set manually. Programmers would write their programs on paper, translate those instructions into patterns of holes on punched cards, and then feed the cards into the machine, which would read the instructions from the cards and execute them.

Although Hollerith tabulators could process census data at blinding speed, modifying the tabulator to process different kinds of data—such as railroad ticket sales—required tediously rewiring the tabulator itself. To address this limitation, the Hollerith tabulator was modified in 1902 to include a plugboard similar to the kind found in old-fashioned telephone switchboards. The tabulator could then be made to tabulate different kinds of data merely by rearranging the plugs.

COMPILERS

Although a punched card may be software, it is a rather unwieldy and limited kind of software. Because its holes need to be relatively big, it can hold only a small amount of information before the card itself becomes impractically large. Punching holes in it requires applying a large amount of force to it with a sharp pin. Although a machine can read information from the holes more quickly than a human can read the equivalent information from paper, the speed at which pins can be pushed through the holes imposes a limit on the speed of any card-reading machine. Finally, and perhaps worst of all, once holes have been punched in the card those holes cannot be erased or changed. Therefore, making even a minor modification to punched-card software requires punching a whole new set of cards.

It was with these limitations in mind that engineers in the 1940s developed magnetic and electronic, rather than mechanical, media for storing data and programs. Today every computer user is familiar with electrical and magnetic storage media in the form of hard disk drives, CDs, flash memories, and the random access memory (RAM) inside personal computers. Such electromagnetically stored software can be stored in a smaller space, be executed more quickly, and be modified more easily than punched-card software.

Although early computer programs were written directly in *machine language*—the binary language of 0s and 1s that computer processors under-

Grace Hopper, a pioneering computer scientist who developed the first compiler for transforming human-readable computer source code into executable machine code, is shown here at the Bureau of Ordnance Computation Project. *(Defense Visual Information Center)*

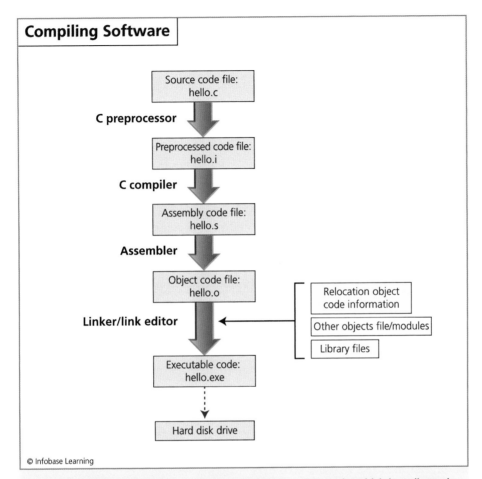

Compiling Software

Source code file:
hello.c

C preprocessor

Preprocessed code file:
hello.i

C compiler

Assembly code file:
hello.s

Assembler

Object code file:
hello.o

Linker/link editor

Relocation object
code information

Other objects file/modules

Library files

Executable code:
hello.exe

Hard disk drive

© Infobase Learning

Computer programmers write computer programs in source code, which is easily read-able and understandable by programmers. Source code, however, cannot be directly executed by computer processors. Therefore, it is necessary to use software called a compiler to translate the source code into machine language code, which is execut-able directly by a computer processor. This diagram shows how a compiler transforms source code file written in the C programming language (hello.c) into executable code (hello.exe) in several stages. The computer's processor can then run the executable code directly.

stand—programming in this way was extremely tedious and time consuming, because it is difficult for programmers to remember that, for example, 0110 is the machine language code for "add" and 0111 is the machine language code for "subtract." As a result, computer scientists eventually developed high-level *programming languages,* such as C, Fortran, Pascal, and Basic, which made it possible to write programs consisting of instructions that more closely resembled mathematical equations and English sentences. High-level programming languages are much easier to write, read, and edit than machine language programs.

The set of program instructions written by a programmer in a high-level programming language is known as source code. Because source code written in a high-level programming language is not written in the machine language code that computer processors understand directly, it is necessary to translate a high-level program into machine language code, known as object code, before the program can be executed by a computer processor. Source code written in most high-level programming languages is converted into object code using a separate program called a *compiler.*

Software compilers rely on the fact that source code is stored in digital electronic form and on the fact that the resulting object code can also be stored in digital electronic form. As a result of such storage, a compiler can read source code from an electronic memory and then write the corresponding object code to the same or different electronic memory. If it were still necessary to implement the final program using a plugboard, the entire process of compiling software could not be performed automatically unless the compiler were connected to a robot that could wire the plugboard at the end of the process.

Before the advent of software-based compilers, human programmers would perform the tedious task of translating human-readable source code into computer-executable machine code by hand using translation tables, much like a human translator might use an English-Spanish dictionary to translate text from one language to another. The creation of software-based compilers automated this task and thereby eliminated the need for it to be performed manually by humans. In the decades since such compilers were first created, programmers have used high-level programming languages to write software to create even more powerful compilers and other tools that have further automated tasks previously performed manually by programmers. Although by doing so, programmers may seem to be programming themselves out of jobs, at the same time they create new demand for programmers with the skills needed to create the next generation of programming languages and software.

Java: Write Once, Run Anywhere

A computer *platform* is a combination of hardware and software that serves as the foundation for all other hardware that connects to the computer and for all software that runs on the computer. For example, the WinTel platform consists of a Microsoft Windows operating system running on an Intel processor (or an Intel-equivalent processor, such as one manufactured by AMD). The Mac platform includes both hardware and software designed and sold by Apple Computer.

Although most platforms can run software that has been

(continues)

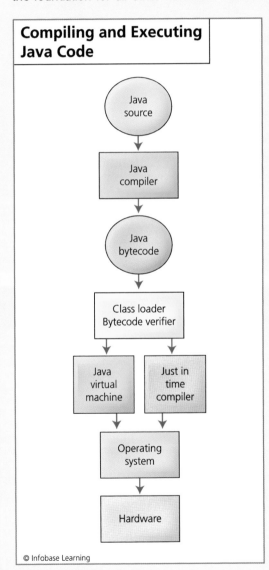

Compiling and Executing Java Code

Java source

Java compiler

Java bytecode

Class loader
Bytecode verifier

Java virtual machine

Just in time compiler

Operating system

Hardware

© Infobase Learning

Source code written in Sun Microsystems's Java programming language can run on multiple computer platforms (such as Microsoft Windows, Mac OS, and Unix) without needing to be rewritten or recompiled separately. Instead, as shown in this diagram, Java source code only needs to be compiled once into bytecode. The bytecode can then be executed on any platform that has a Java virtual machine installed on it. This simplifies the programmer's task of creating software for multiple platforms.

001101010010100111010110101010101011001010100001

(continued)

written in any programming language, differences among platforms often make it necessary to write several different versions of any program, one for each platform. For example, one platform might support mice with two buttons while another platform might support only mice with one button, necessitating that software be written somewhat differently for each platform.

Sun Microsystems introduced the *Java* platform to the public in 1994 in an effort to make it possible to write only one set of source code for any particular program and to use that one set of source code to automatically create software that could run on any platform, leading to the slogan: "Write once, run anywhere." Programs written in Java can achieve this *cross-platform compatibility* because their source code is not compiled directly into object code, but instead into an intermediate kind of kind called *bytecode* that is not tailored to any particular platform. To run the bytecode on a computer having a particular platform it is only necessary to install a collection of software known as the *Java runtime environment* tailored to that platform on the computer. Any computer that has a Java runtime environment installed on it can run any Java bytecode, regardless of the computer's platform.

Although Java has not achieved the universal adoption originally wished for by Sun, it is widely used to program Web sites so that they will be viewable and retain their full functionality regardless of the computer platform that a user uses to browse the Web site.

001101010010100111010110101010101011001010100001

OBJECT-ORIENTED PROGRAMMING

Most early programming languages were *procedural programming languages,* which meant that they consisted of instructions that spelled out sequences of operations to be performed by a computer, much like a recipe provides instructions to be carried out by a chef. For example, a simple program for calculating the length of the hypotenuse of a right triangle according to the Pythagorean theorem ($c=\sqrt{(a^2+b^2)}$) might contain the following instructions: (1) $x = a * a$; (2) $y = b * b$; (3) $z = x + y$; (4) $c = \sqrt{z}$.

Procedural programming languages work well for automating processes that are easily described as a predictable sequence of steps. Not all processes fit this mold, however. For example, consider a word processor, such as Microsoft Word, which does not follow a predetermined sequence of steps. Instead, it must be capable of responding to whatever input the user provides to it at any time, and such input may take a wide variety of forms. If the user types a letter or number, Word must add that character to the current document and display it to the user. If the user clicks the print button, Word must display a window containing print options for the user. If the user clicks the close button in the upper-right corner of the window, Word must close itself. These sequences of events may occur at any time and may be performed in any sequence. Therefore the programmers of Word cannot preprogram it to perform or expect any particular sequence of events in the way expected by programs written in procedural programming languages.

Object-oriented programming languages were developed to address these and other problems. At its heart, an object-oriented program defines a set of program *objects* instead of program procedures. Each object is designed to perform a particular task. For example, the character input object in Microsoft Word might be designed to respond to typing of individual alphanumeric characters on the keyboard; the print object might be designed to display print options in response to the user's selection of the print button; and the exit object might be designed to quit (exit from) Word in response to the user clicking on the close button or hitting Alt-F4. Critically, each of these objects may be programmed to be triggered to execute automatically in response to detection of its corresponding event, such as the typing of a character, the clicking of a print button, or the clicking of a close button.

The code within each such object resembles the code that a programmer would write in a procedural programming language. What is different in an object-oriented program is that the program is organized around objects and the interrelationships among them. This makes object-oriented programming particularly well suited for use in modern computer operating systems, which must be capable of responding to any input provided by the user and any data received from other devices (such as hard disk drives, USB keys, and network cards) at any time.

This does not mean that object-oriented programming has replaced procedural programming. Procedural programming is still useful for performing a wide variety of functions. For example, a program written in a procedural programming language is a perfect fit for a program that runs an accounting report automatically at the end of each month. Furthermore, as mentioned above, the code within objects in an object-oriented program resembles code in procedural programs. Therefore today's programmers must be knowledgeable about both procedural programming and object-oriented programming to succeed in the job market.

INTEGRATED DEVELOPMENT ENVIRONMENTS

Programmers use a variety of software to assist them in writing computer programs, such as:

- *text editors,* which are like word processors but with special features tailored for programming, such as the ability to display an error message if the programmer writes an instruction that is not valid within the programming language in which the program is being written;
- compilers for translating source code into object code (see previous section on compilers on page 75);
- *linkers* for linking multiple object code files together to create larger programs;
- *debuggers* for helping to locate and fix program bugs; and
- *graphical user interface (GUI) builders* for designing the windows, menus, dialog boxes, and other visual components that are displayed by software to interact with the user (see the next section on GUI builders).

In the early years of computers, programmers need to launch and control each piece of software separately. For example, if the program that a programmer was writing crashed, the programmer would need to manually launch a debugger and provide the debugger with information about the program to debug. This was inefficient and frustrating for programmers.

In response to this problem, software vendors developed *integrated development environments (IDEs),* which are computer programs that act as a centralized repository and control center for all of the software that a programmer needs to use to write, debug, and maintain software. For example, an IDE might contain (or be connected to) a text editor, compiler, linker, debugger, and GUI builder that the programmer can access from a single screen. If the programmer has finished writing source code using the text editor, the programmer can just issue a compile command from within the IDE to launch the compiler to compile the source code into object code. If the programmer runs the object code and it crashes, the IDE can immediately and automatically launch the debugger to begin the process of finding the bug that caused the crash. The programmer can design a menu using the GUI builder and use the IDE to make that menu immediately available for use within the program being written by the programmer.

Although some IDEs include their own text editors, compilers, and other programming tools, some IDEs allow the programmer to pick the individual tools to use within the IDE. For example, if a programmer has a favorite text editor that is capable of displaying a list of all instructions that are available within a programming language, the programmer can instruct such an IDE to use that text editor to edit source code. The benefit of such an IDE is that it gives the programmer the freedom to use the best individual tools according to his or her own judgment, while automating interactions among all of the tools selected by the programmer. For this and other reasons, an IDE is an essential tool for every working programmer.

GRAPHICAL USER INTERFACE BUILDERS

From the dawn of computing until around the 1970s, most computer programs were written solely using textual source code containing instructions such as ADD, SUBTRACT, and PRINT. These instructions were particularly well suited to creating software that itself provided only text as output. However, as demand grew for software that could display graphics, and as the ability of computer hardware to display graphical user interfaces increased, it became increasingly difficult to write programs solely using textual instructions. For example, writing instructions to display even a box with an X inside of it might require several lines of textual instructions, such as DRAWBOX (100, 50, 10, 10); DRAWLINE (102, 52, 8, 8); DRAWLINE (106, 52, -8, 8). These instructions were both difficult to write and very confusing even for trained programmers to read. Drawing a window with many menus, buttons, and icons might require writing hundreds or thousands of such instructions.

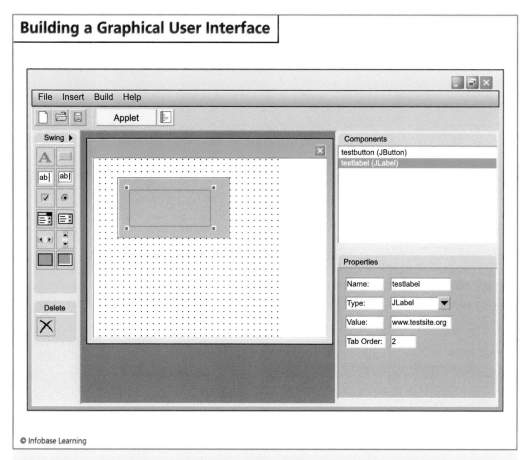

Building a Graphical User Interface

© Infobase Learning

Most modern software uses a graphical user interface (GUI) to interact with the user. GUIs contain visual elements such as windows, menus, buttons, checkboxes, and drop-down lists. Designing a GUI by writing code to describe it would be tedious and time consuming. Therefore, programmers create GUIs by drawing them using GUI design software, as shown in this illustration. The programmer can use a keyboard and mouse to select GUI elements such as buttons and text boxes and to arrange such elements on screen as desired. The programmer then only needs to write code to control how the GUI elements should behave.

Graphical user interface (GUI) builders were developed in response to this problem. A GUI builder is a piece of software that allows programmers to create GUI components—such as windows, menus, checkboxes, text fields, drop-down lists, and buttons—by drawing those components directly on screen instead of by writing instructions defining those components. As a programmer draws

100111010010101010011001011101101010100101001

Edsger Dijkstra, Influential Computer Scientist

Edsger Dijkstra (1930–2002) was a Dutch computer scientist who achieved widespread recognition among computer professionals as a pioneer both in the development of software algorithms and in the transmission of understanding about computer science to the public and to other disciplines.

Unlike many programmers and engineers who are satisfied to do their technical work and to communicate only with others in their own field, Dijkstra was a prolific writer who sought to speak not only to other computer scientists, but also to mathematicians, scientists, and engineers in other fields and to the general public.

Edsger Dijkstra (1930–2002), a Dutch computer scientist, received the prestigious Turing Award in 1972 for making important contributions to the design of computer programming languages. *(HR/UT)*

He was often critical of bad practices and habits within computer science and pushed his peers to improve both their own skills and the software they developed. For example, in 1968, he wrote a letter to the editor of the *Communications of the ACM,* the premier publication of the world's leading professional association for computer scientists, in which he criticized the frequent use of the go to statement in programming languages. The letter, which was entitled "Go To Statement Considered Harmful" by the journal's editors, continues to be cited and used as a model to this day because it provided a subtle but devastating critique of a common programming practice concisely, using easily understood examples and logic, and by appealing to goals that were widely shared among computer scientists. Dijkstra's decision to frame his analysis in this way, rather than

(continues)

100111010010101010011001011101101010100101001

(continued)

as a dense technical paper, was likely a key factor in enabling his argument to reach and convince a broad audience of computer scientists.

Dijkstra is also well known for his sense of humor and for the quotable phrases included in many of his writings, such as:

- "Testing shows the presence, not the absence, of bugs."
- "The question of whether Machines Can Think . . . is about as relevant as the question of whether Submarines Can Swim."
- "Simplicity is a great virtue but it requires hard work to achieve it and education to appreciate it. And to make matters worse: complexity sells better."
- "When we had no computers, we had no programming problem either. When we had a few computers, we had a mild programming problem. Confronted with machines a million times as powerful, we are faced with a gigantic programming problem."
- "If you want more effective programmers, you will discover that they should not waste their time debugging, they should not introduce the bugs to start with."

Dijkstra was recognized for his long-standing and extensive contributions to computer science in 1972, when he was awarded the prestigious Turing Award by the Association for Computing Machinery for his fundamental contributions to developing programming languages. He is missed not only for his technical contributions but also for his humility and training of several generations of computer scientists in his role as a professor at the Eindhoven University of Technology and the University of Texas at Austin.

components using a GUI builder, the programmer can assign a name to each component, such as PRINT_BUTTON or SAVE_BUTTON. The programmer can then write conventional textual source code that refers to those buttons by name, such as code that prints the current document if the user clicks on the button named PRINT_BUTTON. This vastly simplifies the programmer's task of creating GUIs.

One beneficial side effect of GUI builders is that software development companies can hire graphic designers without any training in computer programming to design most of the visual aspects of their GUIs for them, because the design can be performed with a GUI builder without needing to know how to write computer source code. Once the graphic designer has finished designing the appearance of the GUI, the result can be provided to a programmer to write the code that interacts with the GUI. The result is both a better-looking GUI and a more efficient division of labor between different employees of the software company.

CONCLUSIONS

Although computer scientists have benefited significantly from the computer revolution in the form of increased job opportunities and work that is always exciting and interesting, they also face one of the fastest changing job markets of any profession. Whereas a home builder might be able to use the same skills on the job for many years, if not decades, a working computer programmer must update his or her skills monthly, if not more frequently, to stay on top of the latest developments and to stay competitive. As the examples in this chapter illustrate, the fact that computer professionals are employed to create technology that automates tasks previously performed manually is a double-edged sword for those professionals. On one hand, the ability to write software that automates manual tasks enables software developers to command high wages, but on the other the fruits of a programmer's labor today may put him or her out of a job tomorrow.

The relationship between software automation and demand for human labor is not, however, always simple. Consider video games as an example. As video games have grown in popularity and as computer graphics hardware has grown more powerful, the demand for increasingly realistic 3-D graphics and the ability of computers to provide such graphics has grown. This has spurred increased demand for highly skilled graphic artists who know how to use the latest 3-D graphic design software to create realistic environments for use in video games. Although the ability of computer hardware and software to automatically render 3-D images might have led one to conclude that human artists would no longer be necessary, the opposite has turned out to be true. Artists who might previously have needed to piece together a living from large numbers of small projects creating artwork for individual magazine advertisements, for example, might now be able to obtain full-time employment for a year or two working on the next release of a popular video game. As this example shows, although automating a particular task using computers may eliminate the need for humans to perform that specific task, the overall demand for human labor may actually increase as a result, if the result of the automation is to create a new need for human labor to perform a related task that computers are not yet capable of performing.

6

LAW: FROM PARCHMENT TO PCs

Lawyers, judges, and other members of the legal profession tend to resist change. Lawyers continue to use Latin phrases, such as *res ipsa loquitur* ("the thing speaks for itself") and *ignorantia juris non excusat* ("ignorance of the law is no excuse"), on a daily basis. Judges still wear long black robes. Contracts, wills, leases, and other legal documents retain pages upon pages of dense *boilerplate* language originally drafted decades, or even centuries, ago.

The hesitancy of many legal professionals to change quickly stems from the aversion of the law itself to rapid change. One reason that laws tend to change only slowly and gradually over time is that if laws changed quickly and significantly, it would be difficult for members of the public to keep up with these changes and to know how to adapt their behavior to stay within the boundaries of the law. Laws also tend to stay relatively fixed over time out of respect for the effort that has been put into creating and interpreting them and a concern that hasty changes might have unintended negative consequences.

Both the law and legal professionals, in other words, tend to be *conservative,* not in a political sense, but in the sense that they prefer not to change unless absolutely necessary. It should not be surprising, therefore, that the rapid rate of change in computer and Internet technology has posed some significant challenges for the legal profession. This chapter explores just a few of the ways in which the law has adapted to changing technology and the ways in which the legal profession continues to grapple with the implications of such technology.

ONLINE LEGAL RESEARCH

Before the advent of searchable legal databases, such as those offered by Westlaw and LexisNexis, legal research was very tedious and time consuming. Lawyers, law students, and judicial clerks who needed to research a point of law pored through books at law libraries and used obscure reference manuals in order to trace court decisions, statutes, and trial transcripts. One common starting point of reference in most law libraries was *Black's Law Dictionary,* which provided both definitions of legal terms and an indexed citation guide that pointed researchers toward relevant cases. Another common reference source was the *Federal Reporter,* a case law reporter that contains every case decided by U.S. courts of appeals in chronological order.

Today, online services such as those offered by LexisNexis and Westlaw have revolutionized legal research. Both services are offered on a subscription basis and can be accessed using any Web browser. Their primary function is to make statutes, court decisions, treatises, treaties, court transcripts, and law review articles easily searchable, readable, and downloadable. Both companies, however, also offer hundreds of databases offering access to nonlegal information, including newspaper articles, radio and television news transcripts, and information about corporations and government agencies. Although much of the information is also available elsewhere for free (e.g., court decisions are available for free on courts' individual Web sites), people pay for the Westlaw and Lexis services because of their ease of use, powerful search functions, the ability to download documents in Microsoft Word and Adobe Acrobat (pdf) formats, and the ability to search across many databases using a single search.

LexisNexis (originally called Lexis) was the first database service targeted at the legal field. Founded in the 1970s, the LexisNexis database contains case law and statutes dating back to the 1770s. Westlaw, created later in the 1970s, offers a comprehensive, proprietary database of case law, federal statutes, public records, and other informative legal resources. Westlaw indexes legal documents according to West's Key Number System. Each of the hundreds of key numbers corresponds to a different legal topic. Each document in the Westlaw database is tagged with one or more key numbers, indicating the topics that are related to each document. Westlaw users can then search the database for legal concepts by key number. Since the goal of legal research is often to find court decisions and other documents that relate to particular legal principles and concepts, the West key number indexing system enables users to find documents that apply a specific legal concept with a relatively high degree of accuracy. Other features include a notification system that indicates whether cases have been overruled by subsequent cases, and a highly customizable interface so that users can view and interact with information according to their personal preferences.

Before the Internet, users needed to install special Westlaw or LexisNexis software on their computers and then use a direct dial-up connection to connect to Westlaw or LexisNexis. After the World Wide Web became available, both companies began to offer Web-based versions of their services. Now both services are offered solely over the Internet. As a result, users no longer need special software to access them and can instead use a standard Web browser or even an iPhone app to access them.

Most important, both companies employ teams of attorneys who read through every new statute, court decision, and other newly published legal document and write summaries of them. These summaries are then appended and hyperlinked to the documents themselves within the companies' databases. Attorneys who are trying to find relevant cases quickly can search and read through the summaries instead of the entire cases themselves. Each company has its own system of categories for organizing these summaries into various kinds of headnotes to make them even easier to search. These summaries, and the systems each company has created for categorizing and linking them to source material, are some of the companies' most valuable assets because they provide a distinct benefit over free databases that legal professionals are willing to pay for.

These services can also be used to easily determine whether one court decision has been subsequently overruled by a later court decision. Such information is tracked by both Westlaw and LexisNexis and stored in their databases, so that when users view a case they can quickly see whether it has been overruled or modified by later decisions. Before computerized databases, determining whether a case had been overruled required searching through a separate system of books designed specifically for this purpose. The most popular system was called *Shepard's Citations Service*. As a result, the process of determining whether a case was overruled came to be known as Shepardizing. After a legal memo, brief, or other lengthy legal document had been written, the task of Shepardizing the document would be assigned to a law clerk or junior attorney, who would spend hours in the law library carefully analyzing the history of each case cited in the document. Now this task can be performed in minutes by clicking a button, which will then indicate whether the holdings of any cases cited in the document have been overruled or modified by subsequent court decisions.

001101010010100111010110101010101011001010000

The Code of Hammurabi

The *Code of Hammurabi* was one of the earliest sets of laws in the ancient Middle East. Before Hammurabi, kings and judges typically ruled by decree. Without written legal standards, each judge interpreted law in his own way. This led to a subjective application of crimes and consequences. Hammurabi codified laws and created one of the first constitutions. Hammurabi's code includes punitive legal standards, such as "If a man puts out the eye of another man, his own eye shall be put out." It also includes some barbaric customs, such as "If a son strikes his father, his hand shall be cut off." There are a total of 282 laws in the Code of Hammurabi. Copies have been found inscribed on baked clay tablets dating as far back as 1700 B.C.E. The primary similarity between the code and modern law is that it was the first time laws were written down for all to see so that people knew what they were and were not allowed to do.

The Code of Hammurabi is a set of laws of ancient Babylonia dated from approximately 1750 B.C.E. named after the Babylonian king Hammurabi who wrote them. The code was recorded in several forms, including on this human-sized stone stele in the shape of an index finger. *(Réunion des Musées Nationaux/ Art Resource, NY)*

001101010010100111010110101010101011001010000

Because of the high price of LexisNexis and Westlaw, they are used primarily by attorneys, judges, and other legal professionals. They are offered for free, however, to law students. Unlike Google and other Web search engines, LexisNexis and Westlaw typically charge their users for each search they perform. As a result, Lexis and Westlaw users tend to think very carefully before performing a search so that it does not need to be modified and run again. A single search can cost as much as a few hundred dollars if it covers a large number of databases. As an alternative to this pay-per-search model, both companies also offer fixed price monthly subscriptions for individual attorneys and small law firms.

As mentioned above, many individual courts also have their own Web sites from which court decisions and related documents can be downloaded for free. Many administrative agencies, such as the U.S. Patent and Trademark Office (USPTO), have their own databases available online for searching by the public. For example, anyone can search the USPTO database for published patent applications and granted patents. Although most information is viewable and downloadable for free, some of it requires payment. For example, certified copies of patents are only available for a fee. The Court of Justice of the European Union's Web site contains searchable databases of published decisions and opinions. The International Criminal Court at The Hague publishes full decisions against persons charged with genocide, crimes against humanity, and war crimes.

Several sites and agencies offer completely free access to legal information. FDsys, a service of the U.S. Government Printing Office, offers a collection of congressional bills, hearings, reports, the budget, and important administrative agency or Supreme Court decisions. LexisONE, a free service of LexisNexis, offers only the last five years of case law.

EXPERT SYSTEMS

An *expert system* is software that is designed to draw conclusions from facts using logic in a way that attempts to simulate how human experts reason. Since lawyers are experts and specialize in drawing legal conclusions about particular factual situations—such as whether a person is guilty of a crime or entitled to an inheritance—based on legal rules, it should not be surprising that expert systems have been used to engage in legal reasoning and even to provide legal services to individuals and companies.

Expert systems are programmed with knowledge about facts and rules that apply within a particular *domain*. For example, an expert system whose domain is tax law would be programmed to know that:

- the marginal federal tax rate for an individual with an annual income below $8,425 is 10 percent, the marginal federal tax rate for an individual with an annual income between $8,425 and $34,200 is 15 percent, etc.
- the long-term capital gains tax rate is 0 percent for individuals in the 10 percent and 15 percent tax brackets and 15 percent for individuals in all other tax brackets
- home mortgage interest is tax deductible

Such an expert system could then be applied to the financial situation of a particular individual to draw conclusions about that person's tax liability. For example, the expert system could conclude based on the knowledge above that an individual whose annual income is $26,000 is in the 15 percent tax bracket. Although this is a particularly simple example, expert systems can apply the same principles to large sets of complex rules that are interrelated and to large numbers of facts. In fact, Turbo Tax and other commercially available tax preparation software packages are examples of expert systems.

Expert systems are most suitable for use in areas of the law that are governed by rigid and clear rules that do not require subjective judgment to apply. Most of the rules in the U.S. tax code fall into this category. As anyone who has ever prepared a tax return knows, however, many rules in the U.S. tax code are not entirely clear (at least to non-tax experts), and some require judgment calls to be made, such as whether lunch with a colleague qualifies as a business expense. The makers of Turbo Tax attempt to absolve themselves of responsibility for such gray areas by merely providing the end user with an explanation of the applicable tax rule and leaving it up to the user to make a decision about how to apply the rule. For an additional fee, users can also have their questions answered by a human tax expert.

Expert systems are not suitable for use in answering legal questions in fields such as constitutional law, tort law, and copyright law, because many of the legal standards in these fields are highly subjective and cannot be programmed into a computer in the form of rigid rules. For example, whether a store owner is liable for negligence when a pedestrian slips and falls on a sheet of ice in front of the store owner's store depends on whether the store owner maintained the sidewalk in the way that a reasonable store owner would. There is no objective definition of reasonable that can be programmed into a computer in the form of a rule. Therefore advice on whether a particular action is reasonable can only be provided by a human attorney based on his or her understanding of the concept of reasonableness as developed by courts over hundreds of years.

DOCUMENT ASSEMBLY

Paralegals are primarily responsible for drafting legal documents, such as rental leases, wills, and other kinds of contracts. Before document assembly software existed, paralegals typed up hundreds of pages of contracts every day. Today, automated document assembly software, such as HotDocs and ProDoc, are widely used within the legal profession to automate the generation of legal documents. Nearly every law office uses some form of document assembly software to avoid manually retyping commonly generated documents.

Most law firms use document assembly software that is installed on their computers to generate documents for their clients. An attorney may review and revise the document before the final version is sent to the client, and the firm bills the client for creating the document and for ensuring that it satisfies any applicable legal requirements. In contrast, some online legal document assembly services, such as LegalZoom, are targeted directly at consumers in an attempt to make it possible for people to create documents such as wills and leases without an attorney. LegalZoom is directly accessible from the Web for a low one-time or monthly fee.

Document assembly software has a number of advantages and disadvantages. The obvious advantages are high speed and low cost. The obvious disadvantages are that software cannot handle subtle or complex situations that require the expert judgment of attorneys based on years of experience. Also, such software must constantly be kept up to date to reflect changes in the law if it is to generate documents that adequately protect the legal rights of clients.

Assembling legal documents requires a document template and a source of information to fill in to the fields in the template. In the simplest case, once the template is prepared with variable fields for customized information, an attorney,

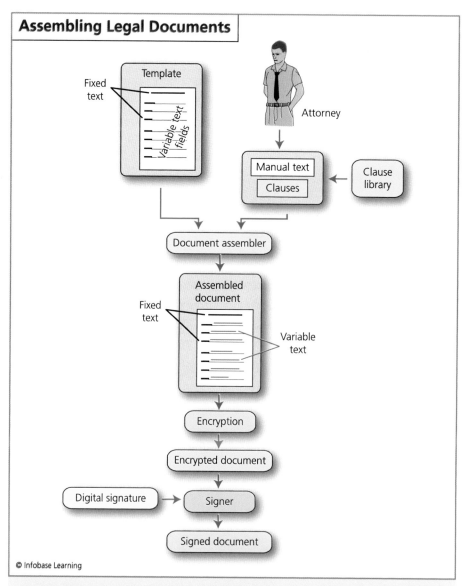

Assembling Legal Documents

Template

Fixed text

Variable text fields

Attorney

Manual text

Clauses

Clause library

Document assembler

Assembled document

Fixed text

Variable text

Encryption

Encrypted document

Digital signature → Signer

Signed document

© Infobase Learning

Attorneys frequently need to generate documents, such as wills and contracts, that differ only in small ways from previous examples of the same kind of document. For example, the will that an attorney writes for one client may include many pages of text copied from the wills of previous clients and contain only a small amount of text that describes the current client's wishes for disposal of her property upon her death. To avoid the need to manually retype or cut and paste the repeated text, attorneys use document assembly software. Because the authenticity of the resulting document may later need to be demonstrated in court, attorneys find it useful to encrypt and digitally sign documents created using document assembly software so that such documents can withstand legal challenges to their validity.

paralegal, or client can manually enter text such as names and addresses or select additional clauses from a clause library provided by the software. Document assembly software then places the text that has been entered—known as variable text—within the placeholder fields in the fixed text and produces a complete document, which can then be printed and signed or encrypted and signed digitally. In some cases, it is possible to pull the variable text from an existing database, thereby eliminating the need for manual data entry, resulting in the automation of the entire document creation process.

Lawyer in a Box

Since the late 1990s, personal *lawyer in a box* software applications such as Quicken Family Lawyer have allowed families and individuals to draft their own legal documents without retaining an attorney, with mixed results. Since legal advice must always be tailored based on the particular facts of each situation, untrained users and complicated legal software often fail to make airtight legal documents. Many users report success when using the software to draft simple legal documents but suggest retaining an attorney for more complicated matters. For example, a married couple with few assets and no children may use Quicken Family Lawyer to successfully draft divorce papers. A husband and wife, however, who each came to the marriage with multiple homes and their own children, who each earned substantial income from multiple sources during the course of the marriage, and who moved from state to state during the marriage, would best be advised to seek the advice of experienced domestic relations lawyers to represent them separately in divorce proceedings instead of attempting to rely on Quicken Family Lawyer.

Quicken Family Lawyer was challenged for engaging in unauthorized practice of law in Texas. The practice of law involves giving legal advice to clients, drafting legal documents, and representing clients in legal negotiations and lawsuits. Without admission to the bar, the practice of law is illegal. According to the original lawsuit, assisting users in creating and filling out legal documents constitutes the practice of law. As a result of the lawsuit, Intuit was at first prohibited from selling the software in Texas, but an appeals court later overturned the decision and lifted the ban on sales of Quicken Family Lawyer.

DOCKETING SYSTEMS

The primary purpose of docketing software is to keep track of the various legal deadlines that apply in a case and to help ensure that these deadlines are not missed. This is both to protect the client and to protect the attorney against engaging in malpractice. Docketing software is used by law firms and in-house corporate legal departments, not by clients themselves.

For a docketing system to work, it must be programmed with the rules that govern deadlines for a particular court or a particular kind of law. For example, patent docketing software, examples of which are PATTSY, FoundationIP, and Case Tracking System, is pre-programmed to know all of the deadline rules for patent law. For example, if a lawyer files a patent application in the United States on January 1, 2012, the software knows that the lawyer has one year in which to file a foreign patent application for the same invention. Therefore, if he or she records the U.S. filing date of January 1, 2012, in the software, the software will automatically generate a deadline of January 1, 2013, for filing the foreign patent application. It will also generate customizable reminders in advance of the deadline. The software can even automatically generate letters to send to clients to remind them about the upcoming deadline.

It is necessary for docketing software to be updated frequently to reflect changes in the laws that are relevant to deadlines. Typically, the docketing software vendors provide this update service for a fee. Making such updates can be complicated because they require analyzing changes in the law, determining how such changes affect any relevant deadlines, and then modifying the software to make sure that it accurately reflects such changes. Failure to make the correct changes to the software can result in failure by the attorney to meet the deadlines, which can result in claims of malpractice against the attorney and loss of legal rights by the client.

Docketing software for use in court cases is used by both courts and by attorneys. Courts use such software to set schedules in cases. For example, after a *complaint* (the document filed by the *plaintiff* in a lawsuit to initiate the lawsuit) is filed, there is typically a fixed period of time in which the *defendant* (the person who is sued) must file a response to the complaint. There is also a fixed schedule according to which subsequent stages in the lawsuit occur. The court can use its software to generate such a schedule and to send the schedule to the plaintiff and defendant, who use their own docketing software to remind them of this schedule and to generate additional items on the schedule for tasks that they need to perform internally.

ELECTRONIC COURT FILING

Despite the growing use of computers in the legal profession, the process of authoring and filing legal pleadings remains a labor-intensive process that has yet to fully benefit from the potential for automation offered by recent advances in computer technology. Efforts are underway, however, to computerize virtually every aspect of court filing and case management. Most courts and government agencies have already supplemented or replaced their paper-based filing systems with electronic filing systems that allow pleadings to be filed over the Internet. Some systems also allow parties to access their case files and the court's docket over the Internet. The Public Access to Court Electronic Records (PACER) service is an electronic resource that allows users to obtain case and docket information from federal, district, and bankruptcy courts.

One significant benefit of electronic court filing is that it can reduce or completely eliminate the problem of lost files. In the days of paper-based files, a courthouse might be filled with thousands of paper files. A judge who was working on a particular case might pull the file and store it on the desk in his office. As a result, the file could easily be lost or simply become difficult for other judges or court personnel to locate. Sometimes files were lost permanently. This could significantly slow down the progress of a lawsuit and cause serious harm to the parties. As a result, law firms took special care to store copies of all documents that were ever submitted to the court in each case so that if the court's file was lost it could be recreated using the files maintained by the parties to the case. Now such problems are becoming a thing of the past. In addition to making it possible to locate all files instantly, it is now possible for multiple judges, attorneys, clerks, and others all to access the complete and up-to-date content of a case file simultaneously, without having to make copies or to wait for someone else to finish making use of a file and return it to the file room.

There are various ways in which documents can be submitted to courts and stored in electronic court databases. The metadata shown in the figure on page 101 includes information about the document being submitted. For example, the metadata might include the contact information for the law firm submitting the document, the name and docket number of the case in which the document is being submitted, information about the format of the document, and the date of submission. It is necessary to generate and store such metadata so that the document can be stored in the correct record in the database and so that the document can later be located when people perform searches on the database.

It is easiest for the court if the law firm that submits the document also creates the metadata and transmits that metadata to the court, because this enables the court's computer system to automatically store all necessary information in the court's database without any human intervention at the court. If the law firm submits the document on paper or submits the document electronically without metadata, then someone at the court must read the document to identify the law firm, the docket number, and other metadata, and then either cut and paste such metadata from the document or type it manually into the court's database.

Courts (and administrative agencies such as the U.S. Patent and Trademark Office) provide various incentives for people to submit documents electronically, such as reduced filing fees and faster processing times for documents submitted electronically. Courts must still accept documents on paper, however, because prohibiting paper submissions would discriminate against people who do not have computers or who are not technically sophisticated enough to generate the required metadata and to perform the electronic submission process. Because courts are public institutions that safeguard individual rights, they must be accessible to all members of the public. However, as computer and Internet access and sophistication become more widespread, and as court electronic filing systems become easier to use, it may actually become simpler and less expen-

(opposite page) Lawyers traditionally have submitted pleadings and other legal documents to courts on paper and in person. Now it is possible to transmit such documents to courts electronically over the Internet, in a process known as electronic court filing. Because courts must be accessible to all members of the public, they cannot require that all documents be submitted electronically. Instead, courts must accept both paper-based and electronic documents. This diagram illustrates how an electronic court filing system processes and stores documents: (1) created electronically and transmitted to the court over the Internet; (2) created on paper and then digitized and transmitted to the court over the Internet; and (3) created on paper and submitted to the court by postal mail. In all cases it is necessary to associate metadata with the document that describes the case with which the document is associated, so that the document can be stored in the correct record in the court's database system.

sive for members of the public to submit court documents electronically than on paper. As a result, at some point courts will likely require all documents to be submitted electronically.

The physical process of filing documents electronically is shown in the figure below. The attorney prepares the document on his computer, typically using

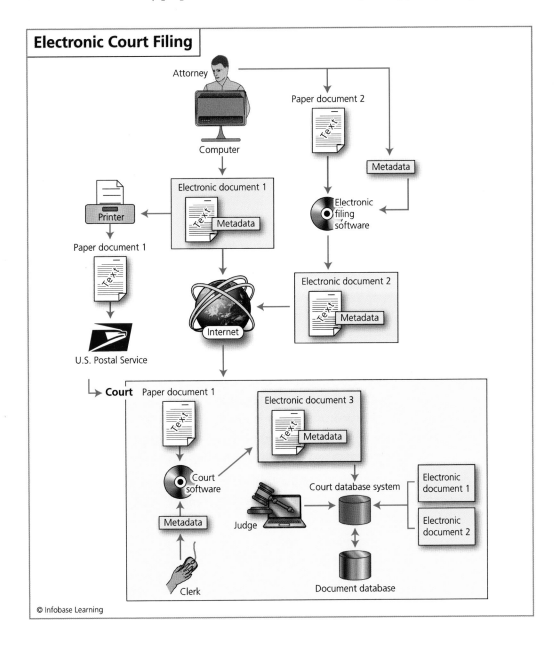

© Infobase Learning

document assembly software, embeds metadata, and submits the document over the Internet to the courts. If the document is printed, the attorney can either scan the document and attach metadata, then deliver the document over the Internet, or print the document and deliver it to the court, where a clerk will attach the metadata by hand. Finally, the electronic document is placed in the court's database system and is accessible by judges, clerks, and parties involved, both through the court's internal network and over the Internet.

ELECTRONIC DISCOVERY

Discovery is a legal process in litigation in which both parties to a lawsuit request information from each other before trial. Discovery includes the following:

- *depositions*—the taking of oral testimony of witnesses
- *interrogatories*—the submission by one party of written questions to the other party, who submits answers to the first party in writing
- *document requests*—written requests submitted by one party to the other party for documents, such as financial records, employment records, and e-mail messages, to the other party, who then provides such documents in response.

Traditionally all of these forms of discovery have been conducted manually and using paper-based records.

Requests for documents can be particularly tedious and time consuming to process. For example, if the plaintiff requests all correspondence possessed by the defendant that relates to the subject of the lawsuit, then the defendant is legally required to scour all of its records for such correspondence and to provide copies back to the requesting party. The defendant, however, can withhold documents that are protected by *attorney-client privilege*. Therefore, responding to even a single request for documents can require the defendant to search all of his or her records, paper files, e-mails, word processing documents, spreadsheets, webpages, etc., to locate documents that are relevant to the request from the plaintiff and then screen out documents that are protected by attorney-client privilege. Even in small lawsuits, this can require attorneys and paralegals to spend hundreds of hours simply to find and copy such documents. Similarly, once the plaintiff receives such documents, attorneys and paralegals for the plaintiff can spend hundreds of hours reviewing them to locate relevant information.

Electronic discovery refers to the process of obtaining electronic information during discovery, such as e-mails and word processing documents. In some cases, information stored electronically is more revealing than paper documents. Meta data, such as time stamps, can show when a document was created or last modified and can be revealing as an important part of evidence. The discovery of electronic data can be more difficult than discovery of the same information stored in a filing cabinet, due to the large volume and transient nature of digital information. There can also be information gaps between a company's attorneys and its IT department, which can result in the IT department accidentally destroying data even after the court has issued an order to cease all document destruction. Another challenge posed by electronic discovery is that electronic data owned by a company may be distributed not only across thousands of computers within the company, but also on laptops, mobile phones, and flash drives in the homes of company employees and on various servers in the *cloud* (such as on Google Docs), thereby making the process of complying with requests for electronic documents particularly difficult.

VIRTUAL ACCIDENT RECONSTRUCTION

Virtual accident reconstruction is the process of using computers to reconstruct automobile and other accidents for use in criminal and civil lawsuits. It often involves using simulators to determine how an accident occurred. It can be used to generate animated three-dimensional videos of an accident to be shown to a jury in a lawsuit. Virtual accident reconstruction is not a new technology. The *energy equivalent speed (EES) method,* which determines vehicles' collision speeds using equations based on the conservation of energy and momentum, has been used for three decades. Today, virtual accident reconstruction is widely used by insurance agencies and courts to determine fault in an accident.

Virtual accident reconstruction allows a presenter to put its audience at the scene of the accident in a three-dimensional virtual reality environment. It can be used to show a judge, jury, and courtroom a video of a reconstructed accident. The technology is particularly useful for showing terrain or road irregularities, peripheral vision, and elevation changes. It can be an excellent tool

Richard Susskind, Author of *The Future of Law*

Richard Susskind is an independent legal technology consultant and author. He is an honorary professor of law at Gresham College, IT adviser to the Lord Chief Justice, chair of the Advisory Panel on Public Sector Information, a columnist at *The Times* (London), and a fellow of the Royal Society of Edinburgh and of the British Computer Society. Susskind's views on the legal profession have influenced lawyers around the world, and his most important work, *The Future of Law,* has changed the way lawyers perceive the field of law.

Richard Susskind is an expert in legal technology who has argued that lawyers who fail to learn to leverage computer technology to work more efficiently will risk being replaced by such technology. *(www.paullawrence photography.com)*

When published in 1996, *The Future of Law* was a groundbreaking text detailing how technology would alter the practice of law. The book brings together specialists in the legal, technology, and public policy fields to illustrate why the failure to embrace technology applications in the legal field will result in poorer legal advice. The book's overarching claim is that law firms in the future will be completely different entities than they are today. Much in the same way that many craftsmen, like cordwainers, wheelwrights, and blacksmiths are no longer viable, Susskind wonders if lawyers might fade from society as well.

To support this argument, he discusses the path a service-based professional industry might take toward commoditization, including "in-sourcing, de-lawyering, relocating, off-shoring, outsourcing, subcontracting, co-sourcing, leasing, home-sourcing, open-sourcing, computerizing, no-sourcing." One might view the work as prophetic, as more than half of these ways to reduce the work of lawyers and automate the practice of law have been invented since the book was published.

for preserving the details of a scene after an accident. Though there are many benefits of virtual accident reconstruction, the drawbacks are significant. For example, there is often a dispute between the parties about the details of virtual accident reconstruction in a particular case, because small changes in how the virtual accident reconstruction is performed can bias the reconstruction toward one party or another.

In many cases, the software applications to perform a virtual accident reconstruction can be installed on a computer at a law firm and used with only minimal training, allowing attorneys to prepare accident reconstruction scenarios in-house.

CONCLUSIONS

Although the practice of law is considered a *profession,* in which lawyers and law firms conduct themselves according to principles and practices that have been developed over hundreds of years, the practice of law in recent decades has felt increasing pressure from outside forces to act more like an *industry* than a profession. Clients, dissatisfied with the high price of legal services and the inability to obtain legal services from anyone who has not obtained a license to practice law, have put pressure on lawyers and the legal system more generally to make more options available at lower prices for satisfying their legal needs. For example, large accounting and consulting firms now often offer tax-related services that traditionally would have been provided only by tax lawyers. Such firms are careful to design such services in a way that avoids constituting the unauthorized practice of law, while still satisfying the needs of their clients for sophisticated tax advice.

Furthermore, as this chapter has illustrated, technologists have worked in cooperation with legal professionals to develop a wide variety of computer software for providing legal services—or the automated equivalent of it—directly to clients, often more quickly and at significantly lower cost than could be provided by a human attorney. Moreover, software is now widely available for use internally by law firms and corporate legal departments to automate many of their routine operations and to decrease the likelihood that errors will be made.

Law firms have felt increasing pressure to respond to these and other changes. As legal professionals find themselves competing both directly with software and

Web sites that offer to solve legal problems for individuals and corporations and as traditional large law firms that employ hundreds of attorneys, legal secretaries, and paralegals face competition from smaller firms able to provide services more efficiently and less expensively by leveraging software and the Internet, it is becoming increasingly difficult for traditional firms to command high hourly billing rates from their clients. As a result, many firms are experimenting with new pricing models, including charging fixed fees for services (such as $1,000 to prepare a will) rather than billing by the hour, billing the client for providing access to online expert systems, and reducing the fees charged to the client in exchange for ownership of stock in the client's company.

Many of these changes are beneficial to the public because they enable legal services to be purchased less inexpensively and more efficiently. At the same time, it is worth considering potential negative implications of these changes for the practice of law as a profession. Traditionally, people have sought lawyers as trusted advisers. This element of trust is enshrined in the requirements that attorneys hold their clients' secrets in the strictest confidence, not revealing them to anyone except in certain very narrow circumstances defined by the law. Furthermore, attorneys are strictly prohibited from representing two clients who have a *conflict of interest.* For example, an attorney cannot represent both the husband and wife in a divorce, because doing so would make it impossible for the attorney to *zealously advocate* for the interests of each spouse without jeopardizing the rights of the other. An attorney representing a client must be able to step into the shoes of that client and make every effort to seek the best possible outcome for that client, without being compromised by the attorney's obligations to other parties.

Certainly this kind of confidence and loyalty are worth something to clients in economic terms. Consumers who buy a mass-manufactured plastic toy for a few dollars understand that the manufacturer's main goal is to sell as many toys as possible for as high a profit as possible. Therefore, when the toy breaks, the owner may be dissatisfied but probably not particularly surprised. Yet legal clients expect and demand more from their attorneys, and rightly so. The requirement that attorneys be experts in their field of law, that they maintain the confidence of their clients' secrets, and that they vigorously defend their clients' interests without being compromised by obligations to other parties is reflected in the relatively high prices charged by attorneys. Therefore, as the legal profession faces increasing pressure from non-law firms and from computer technology and the Internet to drop their prices, those who purchase legal services must at least question whether the lower prices they obtain may also result in a loss of some of the values that both lawyers and their clients have most cherished.

7

MEDICINE: DOCTORS ENTER THE DIGITAL AGE

Medicine is one of the oldest professions and has had a complex relationship with technology. On one hand, doctors often are at the forefront of science and technology. They test new drugs and medical techniques and apply the scientific method to determine which treatments are more effective. Surgeons have both developed and used a variety of innovative tools for fixing and molding the human body to cure diseases and mend injuries. Doctors often are inventors of medical technology.

On the other hand, doctors can be resistant and stubborn in the face of new technologies that could improve the quality of medical care and the health of their patients. When the Hungarian doctor Ignaz Semmelweis (1818–65) first proposed the theory that microscopic germs were the cause of certain diseases and that the incidence of these diseases could be significantly reduced by doctors adopting the simple practice of washing their hands, the medical profession scoffed at what they considered to be an outrageous idea. As another example, many doctors continue to write prescriptions for drugs in illegible print, despite the numerous deaths that occur every year as a result of incorrectly filled prescriptions. Doctors, like others, may have a tendency to hold fast to the practices that they were taught in medical school, even long after they have become obsolete and been proven to be harmful to human health.

This chapter explores just some of the ways in which the medical profession is being transformed by computers and the Internet and the benefits and challenges associated with the use of digital technology in medicine.

ELECTRONIC MEDICAL RECORDS

Electronic medical records (EMRs) are digital records of patient history, prescriptions, and allergies used by hospitals in lieu of paper records. Storing medical records electronically

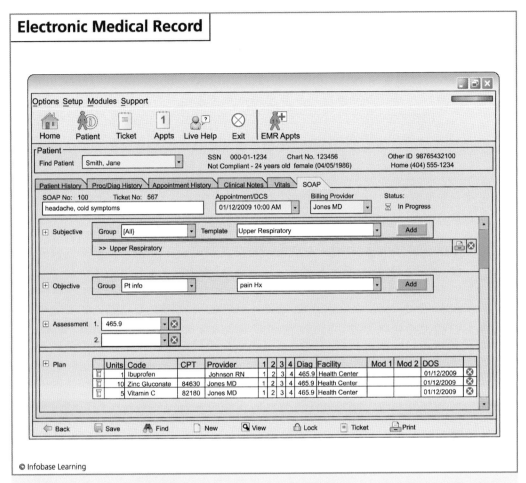

Electronic Medical Record

An electronic medical record (EMR) stores information that previously was stored in paper files, but in an electronic format that can easily be searched, edited, analyzed, and shared among physicians and other medical personnel. Such records can be used not only to maintain more complete records about patients, but also to avoid prescribing harmful medications, to spot potentially dangerous trends in health conditions, and to enable patients to switch doctors without losing important health information as a result of the transition.

allows doctors at different hospitals to maintain up-to-date medical records whether a paper file is available or not. Other drawbacks of paper documents include that records can get lost and damaged, doctors' handwriting can be difficult to read, information is spread out across many pages of paper, and it is difficult to transfer files from one doctor to another. Studies estimate that electronic medical records improve overall efficiency and that the costs of maintaining records in electronic form are offset by the savings associated with preventing unnecessary tests and admissions. The increased portability of medical records, however, also increases the likelihood that they will be stolen by unauthorized users and used to commit medical identity theft.

EMRs can enable medical services to be provided more quickly, when combined with other kinds of computerized medical care. For example, in the past

Privacy of Medical Records

Many people expect their medical records to be kept private, deserving of the strongest protection that the law can offer. Long-standing laws and the age-old tradition of *doctor-patient confidentiality* have protected paper records for many years. The *Health Insurance Portability and Accountability Act (HIPAA),* adopted by Congress in 1996, was an attempt to codify and improve national requirements for the privacy of medical records in the digital age. HIPAA requires health care providers, health clearinghouses, and health insurers to secure any medical records that are transmitted in electronic form. HIPAA also requires doctors to provide patients with access to their own medical records, which was not a requirement before the adoption of HIPAA. HIPAA also provides the patient with legal recourse if the patient's medical privacy has been violated.

HIPAA, however, has a variety of shortcomings, which are a result of attempts to balance patients' interests and those of other stakeholders in patients' medical history, such as the government, hospitals, insurance companies, and related businesses. For example, a patient's consent is not required to release the patient's medical records if the information released is used for treatment of an illness; one would not expect an ambulance driver to get consent before pulling up a victim's medical record and starting treatment. On the other hand, since a patient's consent is not required for billing-related operations, the patient's hospital could submit a claim to the patient's insurance company without the patient's consent, even if the patient would have preferred to pay for the procedure himself. The health care operations that are excluded from HIPAA have broad definitions and include much of a patient's medical record.

it could take several weeks to obtain the results of an X-ray because the X-ray image had to be developed, possibly shipped to a radiologist, reviewed by the radiologist, and the radiologist's report had to be typed up and transmitted to the patient's doctor. Now, an X-ray can be taken directly in digital form, transmitted and reviewed immediately by a radiologist who can type his or her report directly into a computer, and the resulting digital X-ray image and corresponding report can be transmitted and linked directly with the patient's electronic medical record. As a result, X-ray results can be obtained in hours or even minutes instead of days or weeks. This also provides a good example of how EMRs can reduce the cost of providing medical care. By eliminating costly X-ray film and the costly equipment needed to develop, store, and transport such film, the cost of taking X-rays can be significantly reduced. Furthermore, because software can be used to automatically clarify the X-ray image before and while it is being reviewed by the radiologist, computer technology can increase the likelihood that tumors, bone fractures, and other abnormalities will be spotted by the radiologist and that the patient can be treated accordingly, before the problem develops into something more dangerous.

TRAINING BY SIMULATION

Like pilots, doctors today train and practice using simulations to handle a variety of unexpected scenarios. Surgeons use simulations to perform complicated surgeries before ever stepping into an operating room. These systems create a real-time interactive computer simulation complete with common tools used by surgeons, such as surgical saws, scalpels, and sutures. Before simulations, doctors practiced intricate surgery using cadavers and through internships in an operating room. These were expensive, slow, and risky methods of training doctors compared to computer simulations, which can be practiced several hours a day with no risk to patients.

Surgeons who train by simulation might see a simulated body of a patient on a computer screen and then perform a simulated brain surgery by using gloves attached to special sensors to move a simulated scalpel and watch the movement of the scalpel in the simulated brain on screen like on a video game. The surgeon can influence what happens on screen and see the results of his actions, such as tissue being cut and blood flowing.

SURGERY

Computers have also found their way into operating rooms across the country. Operations that require a surgeon skilled in a very specific technique can be performed using *distance surgery,* in which a doctor wears special gloves or moves some other controller in one location to control a robot to perform surgery on a patient in another location. Distance surgery is also seeing applicability in war zones, where doctors are in short supply and not able to be at every operating room at the same time. The earliest remote surgery occurred in 2001 when a surgeon in New York removed a Frenchman's gall bladder. In the near future, if a medical situation can be scanned, converted to digital information, and sent to a remote location, the physical absence of a qualified surgeon or pathologist will no longer be a barrier to care.

Advances in robotics have allowed doctors to engage in minimally invasive laparoscopic surgery in which an incision is made in the leg or elsewhere without cutting through the abdomen or chest. A *laparoscope* equipped with a video camera and surgical tools is snaked to the site of surgery where the doctor operates the tools with a joystick.

Computer-assisted surgery is a surgical revolution that involves the use of a robot to perform surgery supervised and instructed by a doctor. This can eliminate errors that are a result of shaky hands as well as help plan and simulate a surgery virtually, before the actual surgery takes place.

IMAGING AND IMAGE ANALYSIS

Neuroimaging is the field concerned with creating pictures of the brain as a diagnostic or preoperative tool. The oldest forms of neuroimaging include *X-ray computed tomography (CT) scans,* which use a series of X-rays to deliver images of the head from many different directions. Though X-rays and CT scans predate computers, modern innovations have greatly increased the speed and resolution of the images produced by such neuroimaging techniques.

Modern imaging techniques, such as *magnetic resonance imaging (MRI),* use magnetic fields, rather than X-rays, to produce much higher quality images of the inner workings of the brain. Since MRIs use strong magnets, they are not appropriate for users with large amounts of surgical steel from previous surgeries. MRIs take two-dimensional slices of a part of the body, but by accumulating multiple slices, they are able to produce three-dimensional images. MRIs are one of the

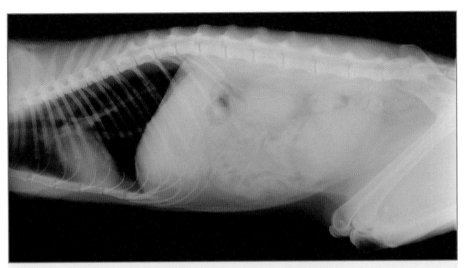

It can be difficult for the untrained eye to spot tumors and other abnormalities in X-ray images. As a result, it has been necessary for skilled human radiologists to interpret such images. Now software exists that can clarify X-ray images and point out regions that require further scrutiny. Such software helps radiologists perform their jobs more efficiently and effectively. The image shown here is a raw X-ray of a human abdomen. *(O and R Technology)*

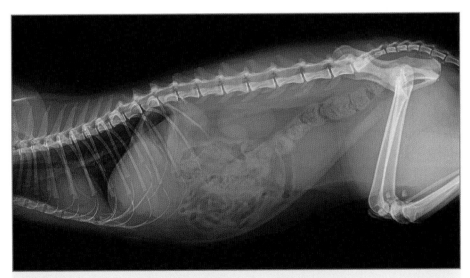

This is the same X-ray as the previous image, after OR Technology's DX-R X-ray clarification software has been applied to it. *(O and R Technology)*

most valuable tools in a hospital, as the resolution they provide is unmatched by other technologies.

Functional magnetic resonance imaging (fMRI) relies on the properties of oxygenated blood to show activation in certain regions of the brain. These regions show up in red or yellow and can allow doctors and scientists to observe which parts of the brain are being used when patients or subjects are asked different questions. An fMRI can be used to detect abnormal blood flow conditions such as ischemia or changes to the brain following a stroke.

Positron emission tomography (PET) scans measure emissions from radioactive chemicals that are introduced into the bloodstream. These techniques allow doctors to determine how much of the radioactively labeled blood is reaching certain areas of the brain and how long it takes.

DECISION SUPPORT

Automated *medical decision support software* can be used to help doctors draw conclusions (such as conclusions about what disease a patient has based on the patient's systems) and prescribe treatments (such as medications based on a patient's illness). Such systems can also help doctors avoid making harmful errors. For example, if the doctor prescribes penicillin to a patient, a decision support system can alert the doctor if the patient is known to be allergic to penicillin or if the patient is also currently taking another medication that is contraindicated with penicillin.

Software such as VisualDX, which helps prevent inaccurate disease diagnoses, has shown to improve diagnostic accuracy by 120 percent. Hospitals and insurance companies like to use this software because it can both help them provide better care to patients and help protect them against malpractice lawsuits.

SPEECH RECOGNITION

Automatic speech recognition is particularly valuable in the medical profession because doctors and other medical professionals prefer to dictate their reports rather than to write them. For example, they like to dictate a report of a visit with a patient immediately after the visit is over, so that they can record the content of the visit and their conclusions before their memory fades, so that they can move

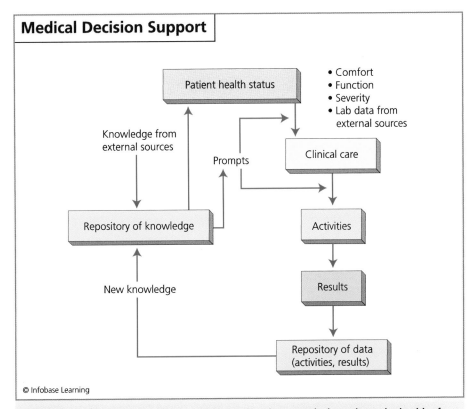

Medical Decision Support

- Comfort
- Function
- Severity
- Lab data from external sources

Patient health status

Knowledge from external sources

Prompts

Clinical care

Repository of knowledge

Activities

New knowledge

Results

Repository of data (activities, results)

© Infobase Learning

Although doctors are trained in medical school to draw conclusions about the health of patients and to prescribe treatments based on all of the available evidence, even the most skilled physicians can overlook possibilities in ways that can have negative impacts on patients. Medical decision support software can be used to analyze electronic medical records and other information related to patients to make suggestions to physicians about diagnoses, medications that should be prescribed, and treatments that should be avoided based on the patient's particular circumstances.

on to the next patient with minimal delay, and so that they do not need to take extra time at the end of the day to write up reports.

Speech recognition for the medical industry faces special challenges. For example, the medical profession uses highly specialized terminology. For speech recognition software to produce accurate transcripts, it must have a dictionary that contains the terms that are likely to be used by speakers. Therefore, speech recognition software must be equipped with special medical dictionaries for it to be useful in medicine. Furthermore, speech recognition software must be highly

001101010010100111010110101010101011001010000

Eliminating Prescription Errors

Prescription errors are a serious problem in the medical industry. One recent study found that 0.4 percent of patients receive the wrong prescription at some point during their hospital stays. Among these, 12 percent involved overlooking allergies, 11 percent were due to incorrect dosages, and 11 percent were due to a misread or miswritten drug name. In another study, researchers found that 30 percent were due to lack of knowledge by physicians, 29 percent to lack of knowledge of patients' medical history, and 30 percent to using the wrong drug name or dosage. Hospitals and insurance companies have an interest in reducing prescription error not only to protect the health of their patients, but also to protect their bottom lines. In 2009, a Pennsylvania woman was awarded $5 million after a medication error led to partial brain damage.

One cause of prescription errors is the fact that most prescriptions are written by hand, and bad handwriting is widespread among doctors. This is particularly dangerous given the fact that many different medications have similar names that can easily be mistaken for each other and that very different numbers can easily be mistaken for each other. For example, confusing a 1 with a 7 can lead to prescribing 700 milligrams of a medication instead of 100 milligrams.

Some technologies that are being used to cut down on prescription errors include speech recognition software, handheld devices that doctors use to type in prescriptions instead of writing them by hand, clinical decision support software, and digital transmission of prescriptions from doctors to pharmacies, instead of using paper or fax (fax transmission can further degrade the quality of a written prescription, making it even harder to read).

001101010010100111010110101010101011001010000

accurate in medicine, because even minor errors can lead to serious problems, such as prescribing the wrong medication or the right medication in the wrong dosage. Despite these challenges, the use of automatic speech recognition is on the rise in the medical industry because of the significant reductions in cost and errors that it can achieve and because it can enable patients to avoid having to wait for weeks or months simply to obtain test results and other information about their treatment.

DRUG DISCOVERY

Drug discovery refers to the process of finding new drugs. In the past, most drugs were discovered by identifying and synthesizing the active ingredient from either traditional remedies or serendipitous discovery. The traditional process of drug discovery is tedious, time consuming, and expensive, with each new drug typically costing several billion dollars over many years to develop.

Morris Collen, Advocate of the Use of Computers in Medicine

Dr. Morris Collen is one of the founding physicians of Kaiser Permanente. He founded it four decades ago with the goal of using computers to improve health care. Dr. Collen created Kaiser's first database in the 1960s, a repository of patient information stored on punch cards, which were used for research purposes. Today, he is recognized internationally for the work he pioneered in applying computer technology to medicine. As an author, Dr. Collen has published more than 180 articles in scientific literature and five books in the areas of preventative medicine, health services research, technology assessment, and medical informatics.

Dr. Morris F. Collen, a pioneer in the use of computers in medicine, shown here in 1968 *(National Library of Medicine)*

Dr. Collen's work helped modernize the medical field with its attempts to move patients' medical records from paper to computers. Kaiser Permanente is credited with one of the first comprehensive prepaid health plans in the nation. Kaiser also leads the nation in the number of Stage 7 Award honors, the award given to hospitals that have achieved the highest level of electronic health record implementation.

Advances in computer technology have promised to significantly reduce the time it takes for researchers to discover new drugs. *Automatic drug discovery,* also known as *computerized drug discovery,* although still in its infancy, can allow companies to evolve and adapt previously known drugs to deliver better drug candidates more cost effectively than the industry's current process.

Software solutions such as those provided by Matrix Pharma use specialized algorithms to perform drug discovery automatically and more efficiently than when using traditional sequential screening. The company's technology mimics the complexity of the human body to evaluate drug candidates based on a large number of variables in order to find the drug candidates most suitable for clinical trials. The platform has led to the development of three new drugs and 11 patents.

CONCLUSIONS

The relationship between doctor and patient is a highly personal one. Doctors become familiar with their patients' most intimate details and often help them to recover from life-threatening illnesses and injuries. A single doctor might attend to the medical needs of an entire family and thereby become almost a member of the family himself or herself. Furthermore, doctors must undergo years of rigorous, often grueling, training to become certified to practice medicine. Perhaps it is because of this combination of a strong focus on personal relationships and a reliance on individual expertise that members of the medical profession—and patients—often are resistant to the introduction of impersonal, automated, computer and communications technology into the practice of medicine.

As the examples in this chapter demonstrate, however, technology need not break the bond between doctor and patient or cause the patient's experience to become one of interacting with a faceless robot. Software that sharpens X-ray images does not replace trained radiologists, but instead assists them in performing their jobs more effectively. Medical decision support software does not absolve doctors of responsibility for deciding which medications to prescribe to their patients, but rather helps doctors to avoid inadvertently prescribing a medication that will have harmful side effects when used in combination with another medication that the patient already is taking. Automatic speech recognition software does not write medical reports, but merely creates transcripts of reports dictated by doctors more quickly and accurately than was possible before.

The use of computers and the Internet in medicine, if applied correctly, need not mechanize and depersonalize health care. Instead, by digitizing medical information, automating mundane tasks, and guarding against errors, digital technology can free doctors and other medical professionals from the need to spend their time on routine and repetitive tasks and instead focus all of their energy on the human work of treating their patients.

8

HOW COMPUTERS ARE CHANGING THE NATURE OF WORK

In agrarian America, most individuals were sole proprietors of their own trade or craft. As the Industrial Revolution began and the assembly line and the factory were created, the way people worked fundamentally changed. For example, instead of a small town being made up of a blacksmith, a farmer, and a doctor, whole towns migrated to a nearby urban center. The benefits of such a move were clear: assembly line labor paid more, schools were better, and there was more entertainment. As a result, though, the newly emerging middle class were trained to work assembly lines, and the assembly line requires a factory, which requires a boss and management. People were no longer the sole proprietors of their own businesses.

Though many corporations still thrive, the assembly line has all but left the United States. The result has been what anyone would expect: a working class spread haphazardly across the continent with few local jobs to match their skills. The invention and subsequent rise of the Internet has provided individuals with the ability to work in both California and New York without ever leaving a home office. Computer technology is reducing costs and providing greater flexibility for both employers and workers. At the same time, computer technology is resulting in increased competition for employers and can result in decreased demand and job security for workers.

OUTSOURCING

Outsourcing is the process of procuring some of a company's goods and services by contracting with an outside supplier. For example, most large manufacturers of consumer

The office lined with indistinguishable cubicles, occupied by workers dressed in blue suits and white shirts, has come to epitomize the concept of the faceless organization man. *(photobank.kiev.ua/ Shutterstock, Inc.)*

products maintain large call centers staffed with customer service representatives who are responsible for handling calls from customers who have questions about the company's products and who require service on the products they have purchased. Many U.S. companies have outsourced such call centers to India, the Philippines, Taiwan, and other countries because of the low cost of wages in these countries. The low cost of international phone calls has made offshore call centers more profitable than call centers located in the United States.

Computer technology and the Internet both facilitate outsourcing of certain types of work because the ability to supervise and communicate with workers in another country at very low cost tip the economic scale in favor of outsourcing work. Outsourcing is particularly attractive to companies when the work itself—such as designing Web sites, writing software, and performing online research—can be performed using computers and be made immediately available without the need to transport any physical product or material overseas.

The benefits of outsourcing from the perspective of the employer include lower costs and the ability to scale up project teams quickly. Some companies also choose to outsource to avoid U.S. taxes, environmental laws, and other regulations that exist in the United States but not in other countries. This aspect of outsourcing has garnered much controversy because many argue that it enables companies to evade legal requirements and mistreat workers in ways that would not be lawful in the United States.

Outsourcing can lead to lower quality work, particularly if the outsourcing company does not sufficiently train its workers or provide them with sufficient supervision. Differences in language and culture between the home country and the country where work is outsourced can also cause problems. Another problem is that products that are manufactured in another country may use raw materials or components that are of lower quality than those used in the company's home country. Such inferior construction can cause products to malfunction and, in extreme cases, can even harm the health of the company's customers if, for example, the materials used in the product are toxic.

Many economists claim that although outsourcing may cost workers in the United States their jobs, it is also the quickest way to bring impoverished countries into the developed world. This difference between the costs and benefits of outsourcing remains one of the most significant sources of tension surrounding the issue of outsourcing.

Although outsourcing was only available to large corporations for many decades, it is now possible for individuals to outsource work, even routine household tasks such as researching products for purchase, buying theater tickets, and planning a child's birthday party. For example, the Web site Your Man in India offers end-to-end personal concierge services for fees as low as a few dollars per task. Service specialists are available for projects as wide ranging as astrology readings or property management. Such services can be purchased over the Web by putting them into a shopping cart and paying online using a credit card much like buying a book at Amazon or a song at iTunes. The only limitation on the tasks that such services can perform is that they cannot require physical presence in the purchaser's location. For example, they cannot provide transportation services or offer to wait at one's home for a repairman, as a traditional concierge service could do. However, as it becomes possible to perform a wider and wider variety of tasks over the Internet, this restriction will become less limiting as a practical matter.

E-LANCING

Freelancers are individuals who are specialists in their field who hire themselves out to companies for work on a project-by-project basis. Writing is one of the oldest professions for freelancers. *Harper's* magazine, founded in 1850, often had much of its content created by freelance poets, authors, and journalists. Freelancing has always been regarded as a low-paying job with no job security, but with the rise of the Internet, there have emerged a number of extremely successful full-time e-lancers (freelancers who perform and/or provide their work online). Since e-lancers can work with clients from all over the world, they do not suffer from the traditional pitfalls of freelancing.

E-lancers are a short-term solution for employers who need to hire someone to fulfill a temporary role on their team. Often, they take on jobs such as Web development for companies too small to need a full-time employee. Since an e-lancer is typically an expert, many companies hire reputable e-lancers for a short time at a fraction of the cost of their annual salary.

Roles commonly outsourced to e-lancers include creative services, such as logo and graphic design, newsletters, copywriting, and video production; IT services, such as e-commerce installation, Web development, and Web design; marketing services, including research, search engine optimization, public relations, and telemarketing; and administrative services, such as data entry, bookkeeping, and virtual assistants or secretaries. E-lancing is best suited for jobs that can be performed from any location (rather than requiring work to be performed on site at the employer's location), that produce work that can be easily transmitted and reviewed online, and that can be done at any time. Some jobs or tasks are not suitable for e-lancing because they require the job to be done on site, such as construction, food preparation, and building maintenance.

Elance.com, one of the most popular e-lancing Web sites, refers to its network of over 300,000 contractors as the *human cloud*. Elance reports that the cumulative earnings of its freelancers has grown roughly 40 percent year-over-year since 2009, totaling more than $27 million by the end of 2010, providing sound evidence that e-lancing is receiving more and more focus from employers and is becoming an increasingly attractive option to workers, particularly those who wish to focus on their specialties and who desire flexible work arrangements.

VIRTUAL COMPANIES

Everyone is familiar with large corporations that have multiple offices spread throughout the United States or even across multiple companies. Today, however, as a result of the low cost of computers and high-speed Internet connection, it is becoming increasingly common even for companies with as few as two or three employees to be distributed across multiple locations, with each employee working in a different state or even country. In such *virtual companies,* each employee performs work at his or her own location and communicates with other employees using Skype, Google Docs, SharePoint, and other software-based communication tools. Although according to traditional wisdom it is more expensive for a company to have offices in multiple locations, the Internet flips this equation on its head. It can be less expensive for the employees of a virtual company to reside and work in separate locations because by doing so they can avoid both moving costs and the need to pay rent for a commercial office space in a high-priced downtown location. Employees in a virtual company often work from home offices or from low-priced office space located in suburbs or rural areas. The employees in a virtual company may meet in person once or twice a year or not at all.

Furthermore, many companies are forgoing the hiring of traditional employees altogether, relying instead on ad-hoc project teams to complete each task independently. This style of teamwork emphasizes fluid, temporary networks of professionals. When the job is finished, whether that is a month or a year later, the team is dissolved and each professional begins seeking new assignments again.

This new breed of lean, online company dispenses with offices and payrolls, which offers many advantages over traditional businesses. Low overhead teams promise lower risks, smaller investment requirements, and a shorter time to market. A wisely spent micro-budget can go much farther than in a traditional business environment. Start-ups with as little as $1,000 in capital can have their products and services branded, set up with a digital product, marketed, and ready to take payments. Starting a business with a low capitalization is called *bootstrapping,* in reference to the maxim that entrepreneurs are capable of pulling themselves up by their own bootstraps.

Companies such as Regus, a leader in *virtual offices,* can provide an individual or company with telephone lines, a mailing address, professional call answering, and conference rooms available to be rented for a low hourly rate, as needed, instead of for a high fixed fee per month. Employees of a company with a virtual office may spend most of their time working in their separate home offices, but convene for face-to-face meetings at a conference room in the virtual office space once a week, or as-needed to meet with clients, vendors, and colleagues. The result is a high-quality office space for only a fraction of the price of a traditional commercial real estate lease, because the company only pays to use the physical office space for a relatively small number of hours per month.

Such a virtual company may appear to the outside world as if it is no different than a traditional company with a permanent physical office, because customers who arrive at the virtual office space to meet with company representatives are greeted by a receptionist and taken to a conference room to meet with those representatives. Yet the company pays only a fraction of the rent for the virtual office that it would pay for a permanent full-time office. Furthermore, if the company hires additional employees, it does not need to increase its real estate expenses. Yet another benefit of virtual offices is that companies such as Regus have offices available throughout the United States. Therefore, if an employee of a company with a Regus virtual office based in New York needs to meet with a client in Boston, that employee can simply book a conference room at a Regus office in Boston, thereby providing the appearance that the company has branch offices in multiple cities.

CROWDSOURCING

The preceding topics of outsourcing, e-lancing, and the emergence of virtual companies all existed prior to the Internet in some form or another. Outsourcing has been prevalent since World War II; freelancing has been around for centuries; and Hollywood has always employed fluid teams of experts that join together temporarily until the production of a movie is completed. Unlike these topics, *crowdsourcing* is an entirely novel way of getting work done. Crowdsourcing refers to asking members of the public to contribute in small ways to a project and then compiling and using the contributions of many people in aggregate.

For example, Amazon's *Mechanical Turk* allows employers to create projects on a scale of their choice and pay users to complete tasks. Mechanical Turk has been used to lower the cost and increase the respondents of a number of projects, including academic studies, user interface design preferences, and crisis response.

An example of the perfect task to crowdsource is a project such as finding the names and e-mail addresses of the CEOs of all of the companies on the Fortune 500 list. Someone who wishes to obtain this information could crowdsource the job by submitting the job description to a crowdsourcing Web site along with an Excel spreadsheet listing the names of all 500 companies. Users then see the job description and the fee offered by the buyer per submission. Any user who is interested can pick a company's name from the list, search for and submit the CEO's name and email address, and then get paid automatically through the Web site—usually a very small fee, such as five or ten cents. They can do this multiple times for multiple names on the list to accumulate more earnings. A project of this size might be completed on the Mechanical Turk site within 30 minutes and cost the buyer less than $100, representing a significant cost savings over hiring a local researcher to perform the same job and sparing the buyer the need to search for and interview multiple candidates before picking one to do the job. Furthermore, because workers across the globe are scouring the Mechanical Turk for jobs to perform 24 hours a day, seven days a week, 365 days a year, someone who posts a job at 3 A.M. on a Sunday might find the job completed just a few hours later, unlike traditional jobs, which might take weeks to initiate and then only be performed on weekdays during working hours.

Some companies, such as CastingWords, use a crowdsourcing platform iteratively in order to create professional transcriptions of spoken audio recordings for clients for extremely competitive prices. A single transcript is first created by an entry-level transcriptionist and then sent for review by seasoned transcriptionists. Transcriptionists who work for CastingWords are paid commensurate with their experience, and the transcriptionists with the highest skill level perform editing, quality control, and final approval.

Companies such as txteagle tap into the human crowd in order to perform on-the-fly translations. For example, assume that a survey needs to be translated from English into Arabic. The txteagle translation service breaks up the text in

`1001110100101010100110010111011010100101001`

Douglas Engelbart, Advocate of Using Computers to Boost Human Ability

Douglas Engelbart (1925–   ) is a pioneer in computer science and human-computer interaction (HCI) who is not well known despite his significant contributions to computing technology. For example, he designed and built the first computer mouse in the late 1960s—about 15 years before mice came into widespread use with the introduction of the Apple Macintosh in 1984. In 1968, he gave a public demonstration of the online system (NLS) that he and his team had been developing. The demonstration has since become known as the mother of all demos among computer professionals because it was so far ahead of its time that it shocked and amazed even the audience of seasoned experts who attended it. In the demo, Engelbart not

Computer user interface pioneer Douglas Engelbart, shown here with a prototype of the first computer mouse *(SRI International)*

only exhibited the computer mouse for the first time in history, but also showed working versions of hypertext and an online videoconference between two people located at different sites. Such technologies would not become mainstream for another 20 to 30 years.

Beginning in the early 1960s, Engelbart formulated and began to pursue a grand vision of "augmenting the human intellect." He viewed computers not as tools that should be designed with the goal of replacing human thought, but rather as tools whose purpose was to augment the intellectual capacity of the human brain. As a simple example, he envisioned interactive word processors (long before they existed) as tools that could supplement limited human memory

(continues)

`1001110100101010100110010111011010100101001`

00110101001010011101011010101010101100101000001

(continued)

by acting as interactive scratchpads that, by making documents easy to edit quickly, would facilitate more fluid and intuitive interaction between the human writer and the word processor than could be possible with pen and paper alone. Engelbart's insistence that computers should supplement human thought, rather than replace it, put him at odds with computer scientists of his day who advocated the goal of developing computers capable of artificial intelligence, which would make human intelligence irrelevant and obsolete.

Engelbart founded Stanford's Augmentation Research Center in order to develop and experiment with tools and technologies meant to augment human interactions with computers. More recently, he and his daughter, Christina Engelbart, founded the Bootstrap Institute, which continues to promulgate Engelbart's ideas about human-computer symbiosis, a half-century after he first began to develop them.

00110101001010011101011010101010101100101000001

the survey into individual sentences, identifies participants who are capable of translating from English into Arabic, and sends those sentences to the identified participants as text messages on their cell phones. The participants translate the sentences they receive from English into Arabic, send the translated text back to txteagle, and receive a small payment in exchange. The txteagle service acquires multiple translations of the same sentence from multiple people to ensure the quality of the translation. Finally, txteagle combines the translated sentences back into the correct sequence to obtain a translated survey. Translating a document that is even 10 sentences long might involve 50 people or more. The participation of all translators in the process is coordinated automatically by txteagle's crowdsourcing software.

CONCLUSIONS

For most of human history, the nature of work did not change significantly from generation to generation. Children entered the same trade as their parents.

Farmer's children became farmers, often taking over the same farm that had been in their family for generations. Sons and daughters of kings and queens themselves became kings and queens. Furthermore, when a child entered the same trade as her parents, most likely she could simply learn the same skills as her parents and then apply those skills to her job for the rest of her life.

In the industrial age this began to change. It became possible to become *socially mobile*—for an individual to be born into one social class and yet enter a different social class during one's lifetime. A working class daughter of a tanner might, through some combination of education, hard work, and luck, enter the middle class as a schoolteacher. No longer did the job or profession of the parent dictate that of the child.

Still, in most cases individuals chose or found themselves in a job and remained in that job or at least the same category of job for their entire working lives. In the 20th century, it was common for an accountant to work at the same accounting firm for 40 years and then retire. An accountant who changed jobs voluntarily would almost certainly do so in order to work at another accounting firm. Changing jobs frequently or changing from one career to another was considered unusual and might call one's judgment and reliability into question.

This began to change as the 20th century drew to a close. By the first decade of the 21st century, employees in the United States had been with their current employer for only slightly over four years on average. Some estimates indicate that students graduating from high school today may hold anywhere from five to seven jobs during their working lives, including at least one major career change.

Even those who stay in the same job working for the same employer for their entire lives must now contend with the fact that the skills required for that job are likely to change significantly over time, in large part due to rapid changes in computer and Internet technology. Because employers, whether in the public or private sector, have strong incentives to use computers and other machines to perform routine tasks instead of paying human workers to perform those tasks, the responsibilities that are assigned to those workers will inevitably change over time as computers become capable of automating a wider and wider variety of tasks. Once a particular task, such as answering a customer's question over the telephone, can be performed automatically by a computer, the person who was previously employed to perform that task can either be put out of work or be

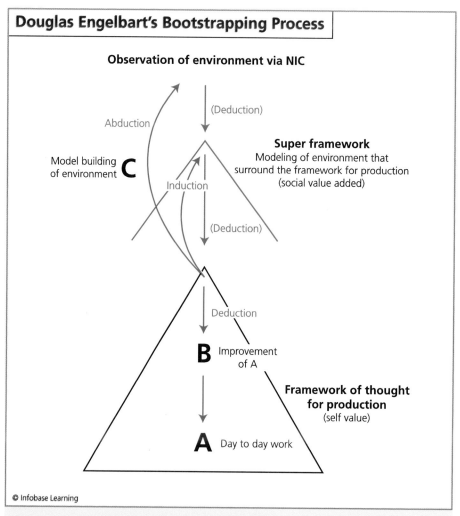

This diagram illustrates Douglas Engelbart's bootstrapping process for continuously improving the process of innovation in organizations.

assigned to new responsibilities, such as verifying the accuracy of the new customer support software or finding ways to improve the software itself.

Workers who are able to adapt to changes in technology and adopt new skills will thrive in the new era of ever-changing work requirements. Workers, in other words, must be ready to retrain themselves and engage in continuous education. No one is more familiar with this cycle than computer scientists themselves, who by constantly inventing new computer hardware and software to automate their own skills must always be capable of developing new skills to design the next generation of computer technology.

Douglas Engelbart uses the term *bootstrapping* to refer to a process by which both individual workers and the organizations in which they work continuously improve the products they produce, the process by which they improve those products, and the way in which they improve the process of improvement itself. In Engelbart's model, type A work is the day-to-day work performed by people in an organization, such as the process of making shoes in a shoe factory. Type B work is the work involved in improving how the organization makes shoes. It is worth noting that many individuals and organizations never make the effort to engage in type B work to improve themselves. An example of type B work in a shoe factory that only purchases leather from a single supplier would be to begin purchasing leather from multiple suppliers to reduce the likelihood that the manufacturing process will ever grind to a halt as the result of a lack of raw materials.

Finally, type C work involves improving the process by which improvements are made to type A work. For example, type C work in a shoe factory might involve developing a system for generating, evaluating, and implementing suggestions for ways to improve the process of making shoes. This might include monthly meetings to discuss ideas for improvements and a committee to evaluate the ideas discussed at the meetings.

Although the example above applies Engelbart's bootstrapping process to the operations of a company, the same principles can be applied to an individual to improve that person's skills and to enable him or her to systematically improve the process by which he or she improves those skills. Whether or not one agrees with the details of Engelbart's approach, his premise is particularly relevant to the universal need of workers in the computer age to proactively upgrade their skills to keep pace with the rapid rate of technological change. Although workers who obtain training in new skills as necessary in response to new technology will fare better than those whose skills stagnate, the workers who truly excel will be those who develop and stick to a systematic and proactive plan for continuous self-improvement.

CHRONOLOGY

250 B.C.E.	Ctesibius of Alexandria, a Greek inventor, invents a water-powered clock with gears and an hour hand
late 1600s	Sir William Petty, an English economist, describes the division of labor in Dutch shipyards
1776	Economist Adam Smith writes that economic growth results from increasing division of labor
1775	The Industrial Revolution begins, and factories mushroom as assembly line technology makes manufacturing faster and easier
1801	Joseph-Marie Jacquard invents the Jacquard loom, which could weave patterns into cloth automatically using specially prepared punched cards that encoded the patterns to be woven
late 1800s	Nicola Tesla, the inventor of AC electricity and radio, develops remotely controlled vehicles
1881	Alexander Graham Bell, his cousin Chichester Bell, and Charles Sumner Tainter invent a recording device with a rotating wax-coated cylinder on which grooves can be cut by a stylus, an early prototype for the Dictaphone
1888	John Robert Gregg devises his shorthand system, which was once widely taught in public schools as an essential skill needed by office workers
	Bell and Tainter form the Volta Graphophone Co. to manufacture machines for the recording and reproduction of sound in office environments
1889	Frederick Winslow Taylor begins a comprehensive reorganization of the manufacturing plant, in which he outlines the duties of every worker, from the company president to the water boy

1890	Herman Hollerith's tabulating machine tabulates the results of the U.S. census; Hollerith eventually founds International Business Machines (IBM)
1899	U.S. secretary of war Elihu Root introduces scientific management to the American military
1902	George Blickensderfer produces the first electric typewriter, but a practical version will not be manufactured until about 1925; it will be the 1950s before the machines gain widespread acceptance
1907	The American Graphophone Co., which later became the Columbia Graphophone Co., acquires the Volta Graphophone patent in 1907 and trademarks it Dictaphone
1908	The Ford Model T automobile makes its debut, selling for $825
1911	Frederick Winslow Taylor publishes *Principles of Scientific Management*
	Congress launches an investigation of scientific management after workers at the Watertown Arsenal in Massachusetts go on strike, but investigators eventually conclude that the system does not abuse workers
1923	Henry Ford famously writes, "Any customer can have a car painted any color that he wants so long as it is black"
1927	Henry Ford builds the first vertically integrated modern factory by purchasing the mines that created the ore, the factories that made the glass, and the plantations that grew the rubber
1944	Howard Aiken designs the Harvard Mark I computer, which could process programs provided to it on punched cards, much like those used by the Jacquard loom
1945	Kaiser Permanente, a company on the forefront of medical informatics, founded to provide care to war veterans

1952	Grace Hopper completes the design of the first software compiler, known as the A-0 system, for use with the UNI-VAC I computer
1957	First compiler developed for the FORTRAN high-level programming language
1960s	Computerized health records conceptualized at the University of Vermont
	United Kingdom grocery giant Tesco uses supply chain management to achieve vertical integration with suppliers and customers, increasing their market share to provide over 30 percent of all groceries sold in the United Kingdom
1961	IBM introduces its Selectric electric typewriter
1962	Joe Engelberger, known as the father of robotics, founds the Unimatics Company, which produces the Unimate, a robotic arm first used for auto assembly by General Motors
1970s	Diagnostic system MYCIN developed to help diagnose bacterial diseases
1971	One-third of all working women in the United States are now secretaries
1972	First laparoscopic surgery performed
1973	LexisNexis legal research system revolutionizes the way legal research and analysis is compiled
	Dennis Ritchie completes the design of C, one of the most popular and influential high-level programming languages
1975	The Westlaw computer-assisted legal research service introduced
1976	A *Business Week* article about a paperless office is written ahead of its time, and the concept is mostly ignored until the 1990s
1980	Smalltalk-80, one of the most influential object-oriented programming languages, released to the public

1980s   Term *supply chain management* coined by a U.S. industry expert in a report calling for a large-scale effort at reengineering supply lines, downsizing businesses, and attention to cost reduction

COSTAR system developed to provide electronic medical records to ambulances

1983   VisiCalc, the world's first spreadsheet program, is released for the Apple II. This software served as a vital tool for business accounting departments, to the point that many personal computers were sold with the single purpose of running the VisiCalc application

Microsoft releases Version 1.0 of Microsoft Word

1984   Apple introduces the Macintosh, the first personal computer to feature a graphical user interface

1988   Electronic public access service PACER, created and managed by the Administrative Office of the United States Courts, allows users to obtain case and docket information electronically

1990s   Globalization of business allows development of multinational corporations with the goal of increasing competitive advantage by reducing costs through outsourcing

1992   The AT&T Voice Recognition Call Processing service is introduced and routinely handles about 1.2 billion voice transactions each year using automatic speech recognition technology to route the calls

1992   Microsoft releases Microsoft Office

IBM introduces the first smartphone, the IBM Simon, at the Comdex trade show in Las Vegas; Simon contains a calendar, address book, world clock, calculator, notepad, fax and e-mail capability, and games

1993   HotDocs document assembly software templates created for use in legal offices

1994	Job-matching database Monster.com founded
	Sun Microsystems releases the Java platform to the public
1996	Richard Susskind's *The Future of Law* details how technology will impact the practice of law
	Health Insurance Portability and Accountability Act (HIPAA) enacted by U.S. Congress to encourage the standardization and use of electronic health care records
	Nokia introduces the first mobile phone with full personal digital assistant (PDA) functionality; the 9000 Communicator will become the world's best-selling PDA and will spawn a new category of mobile phones—the smartphone
1997	LexisNexis creates Web-based search engine for its legal research database
1998	Westlaw.com founded, providing access to the Westlaw database via the World Wide Web
	Harvard Business Review publishes an article entitled, "The Dawn of the E-Lance Economy," spurring the development of several Web sites devoted to enabling people to hire e-lancers and to enable e-lancers to find work
1999	Salesforce.com founded by former Oracle executives to host software as a service (SaaS) customer relationship management (CRM) products
2000	LegalXML Electronic Court Filing Technical Committee creates technical specifications to standardize the electronic filing of court documents
	Virtual office provider Regus completes a successful IPO on the London Stock Exchange
2001	LegalZoom begins offering boilerplate legal documents, such as contracts, wills, and intellectual property registration, to the public

First distance surgery performed by a surgeon in New York on a patient in France

2002   Online freelancing site Elance created

2003   Social networking site LinkedIn founded as a networking site for employers and employees

2004   Advances in robotics due to corporate and military research allow iRobot to introduce the first Roomba, a floor cleaning robot

2005   Amazon's Mechanical Turk online crowdsourcing platform launched publicly and, within days, tens of thousands of Human Intelligence Tasks (HITs) are registered and completed

2006   Article entitled "The Rise of Crowdsourcing" explains how technological innovations can allow companies to take advantage of the talent of the public

2007   Apple's revolutionary iPhone is released along with productivity suites, enterprise-ready software, and a developer SDK that allows companies to build custom apps to suit their business needs

Caterpillar develops and tests a dump truck driven by a robot and requiring no human interaction

2009   Princeton and Harvard create the RECAP service, a free alternative to PACER

2009   Use of electronic medical records by office-based physicians rises to 48.3 percent, up significantly from 38.4% percent in 2008

The American Recovery and Reinvestment Act of 2009, also known as the stimulus, includes a $20 billion grant to medical facilities for electronic medical records

First virtual surgery performed on a simulator, allowing surgeons to practice prior to the actual operation

Hackers steal 160,000 electronic medical records of faculty and students at the University of California, Berkeley

2010

Organovo, Inc., uses a 3-D printer to automatically construct blood vessels from individual cells, with the goal of eventually using artificial blood vessels for human arterial grafts and other medical procedures

Etsy, a Web site that allows individuals to sell handmade or vintage items, grows to 7 million registered users and estimates $400 million in annual transactions

Overwhelming demand for the iPhone 4 causes supply issues for Apple, widely regarded as a leader in supply chain management

Salesforce.com, a customer relationship management platform, finds widespread adoption, causing the value of its stock to increase by 400 percent over 24 months

President Obama's landmark Patient Protection and Affordable Care Act forces hospitals to comply with modern electronic medical record systems such as Epic, McKesson, Cerner, and MediTech

Robotic surgery experiences explosive growth, growing from 210 installations in 2003 to 1,395 systems in 2010

2011

Txteagle service leverages the mobile phone networks in developing countries to crowdsource tasks such as translation

Sales of industrial robots rebound and are expected to reach 143,000 units annually by 2015, as manufacturing companies seek to reduce costs and increase efficiency

A team of engineers and chefs collaborates to use 3-D printers to assemble pureed foods into edible objects having complex shapes, such as miniature space shuttles made of ground scallops and cheese

Blueprints for high-precision 3-D fabrication machines, along with thousands of CAD files containing common objects, allow individuals to design and print everything from plastic silverware to toys from their home computer

Industrial robots formerly used by the automotive industry find a new home in recycling plants when developers create artificial intelligence algorithms for sorting through garbage

Police use crowdsourcing to identify rioters and looters following the Stanley Cup finals in Vancouver

GLOSSARY

accessorizing a customization approach that allows customers to add features to a core product, such as the applications users can purchase for iPhones

affiliate an owner of a Web site who participates in an online retailer's affiliate program and who provides Web-based advertisements that direct users back to the retailer's Web site in exchange for a commission

affiliate program a program used by online retailers to pay commissions to other Web sites that use advertisements to direct users back to the retailers' Web sites

application service provider (ASPs) a business that provides software-based services to customers over the Internet

assembly line a manufacturing technique in which a product is transported by conveyor to successive stations at which various assembly steps are performed

attorney-client confidentiality a legal rule that protects the confidentiality of information obtained by a lawyer about the lawyer's client; lawyers are not allowed to reveal client confidences except in extreme situations specifically authorized by the law

attorney-client privilege a legal rule that prohibits one party to a lawsuit from obtaining information about communications between the other party and that party's attorney

automatic drug discovery the process of discovering new drugs automatically using computers, usually by simulating new drugs; automatic drug discovery can significantly reduce the cost and time required to discover new drugs

automatic process control the practice of using computer technology to operate power plants and factories more efficiently and safely through the automated regulation of mechanical systems

automatic speech recognition technology that automatically recognizes spoken words for the purpose of creating documents or controlling a computer

banner advertisement   a form of advertisement which takes the form of a rectangle filled with text and/or graphics on a webpage

behavioral tracking   a method used by online advertisers to identify a user's interests based on the Web sites that he or she has visited in the past

Black's Law Dictionary   a legal reference book published in the late 19th century and widely considered by lawyers and judges to be an authoritative source of the meanings of legal terms

boilerplate   text that can be used in multiple documents without being modified from the original; large amounts of boilerplate text are often used in wills, contracts, and other legal documents

bootstrapping   from the maxim "to pull oneself up by one's bootstraps," refers to the act of an entrepreneur starting a business with little or no initial capital and growing that business based on revenues generated from customers, with little additional outside investment

business process automation   using software and the Internet to enable business processes, such as generating invoices, performing accounting audits, and approving contracts, to be performed automatically or with minimal human intervention

business process modeling   using software to create flowcharts and other digital models of the processes performed within a business so that employees of that business can better understand how those processes are performed and to improve the processes themselves to make them more efficient and effective

bytecode   the form that Java programs take after being compiled by a Java compiler; Java bytecode can be executed on any platform on which a Java run-time environment is installed

call center   a centralized office used for receiving and making large numbers of telephone calls on behalf of a business or other organization, often to perform sales, marketing, bill collection, customer service, and technical support functions

check-out/check-in   a feature of many document management systems that allows only one user at a time to alter a document, preventing the creation of overlapping versions

cloud   information and software stored on the Internet rather than on a computer; Google Docs is an example of software provided in the cloud that also stores documents, spreadsheets, and other data

Code of Hammurabi   a set of Babylonian laws carved into stone; one of the earliest written constitutions

compiler   computer software that translates human-written source code into object code so that the object code can be executed by a computer processor; software purchased and downloaded over the Internet for installation on a computer

complaint   the document filed by the plaintiff to initiate a lawsuit in court

computerized drug discovery   see AUTOMATIC DRUG DISCOVERY

conflict of interest   a situation in which two clients of an attorney have interests that are in conflict with each other, as in the case of a husband and wife engaged in divorce proceedings; attorneys are prohibited from representing two clients if doing so would pose a client of interest between those two clients, with only narrow exceptions

conservative   a preference for rules, customs, and ethics to remain the same over time

contextual advertising   the process of selecting advertisements that are relevant to the content of a webpage by scanning the webpage for keywords and then displaying advertisements related to those keywords; a webpage containing a recipe for cookies might display a contextual advertisement for a book of cookie recipes

craft production   the process of making products by hand; the most common manufacturing method in the preindustrialized world

cross-platform compatibility   the ability of computer hardware or software to work in conjunction with multiple computer platforms

crowdsourcing   the act of outsourcing tasks to the public to be performed in small chunks by many different people

customer relationship management (CRM)   processes implemented by a company to handle its contact with customers; now often managed and at least partially automated by software such as that provided by SalesForce.com

debugger   software that assists programmers in finding and fixing bugs in source code

defendant   the defending party in a lawsuit

demographic ad targeting   a method used by online advertisers to identify a user's interests based on demographic information that they have supplied themselves, such as their age, gender, and home zip code

deposition   out-of-court testimony by a witness as part of discovery

digital fabricator   a self-contained factory that can make objects described by digital data; works on the same principles as a desktop computer printer, but produces three-dimensional, solid objects

direct model   a business model in which a company sells directly to the consumer rather than through retailers; Dell Computer was responsible for popularizing the direct model in the computer industry

discovery   the pre-trial phase in a lawsuit in which the attorneys for both parties obtain information from each other that is relevant to the lawsuit; some lawsuits are settled solely as the result of discovery, without the need for the case to go to trial

discrete circuits   electronic circuits that contain separate components, such as resistors and transistors, instead of a single integrated circuit; forerunner of integrated circuits

diskette   a flexible plastic magnetic disk used to store data or programs for a computer; forerunner of the CD-ROM and flash drive

distance surgery   technology that allows surgeons to perform surgery on a patient even when the surgeon is not physically present in the same location as the patient

division of labor   the process in which each worker specializes in learning and performing only a single repetitive task and each task combines to produce a completed whole

doctor-patient confidentiality   a legal rule that protects the confidentiality of secrets shared between doctor and patient during the course of providing medical care

document assembly software software that is used to automatically create multiple versions of the same letter, invoice, invitation, or other document, where each copy contains largely the same text, with only minor differences, such as the name and address of the person to whom the document is addressed

document management system an electronic system that organizes and manages documents, tracking multiple versions and allowing access to multiple users

document request a set of requests provided by one party in a lawsuit to the other party for specific documents as part of discovery

domain a particular field of knowledge, such as law, science, art, or religion; computerized expert systems typically are only programmed with knowledge within a particular domain and therefore can only draw conclusions about situations within that domain

dot-matrix printer a printer that uses hammers and a ribbon to form images out of dots

drug discovery the process of discovering, testing, and synthesizing new drugs

electronic medical records (EMRs) medical records stored in computer databases or other electronic form, rather than on paper, so that they can be created, edited, and transmitted more easily among doctors, patients, insurance companies, and other parties who are entitled to access such records

energy equivalent speed method a set of equations that can be used to determine a vehicle's speed at impact in an accident based on the amount of damage to the vehicle; often used for virtual accident reconstruction

expert system software that uses artificial intelligence to simulate the knowledge and decision-making processes of human experts

Federal Reporter a publisher of decisions of the U.S. courts of appeals, widely cited in legal documents

field in a database, a portion of a record that is dedicated to storing a particular kind of information, such as a person's name, address, or telephone number

fixed text portions of a template-based document that remain unchanged from one instance of the document to the next

Fordism   an adaptation of Taylorism that aimed to increase productivity by standardizing output, using conveyor-belt assembly lines, and dividing work into small, simple tasks; named for Henry Ford, founder of the Ford Motor Company

freelancer   a self-employed individual who works on a contract-by-contract basis in fields such as writing, Web design, and marketing

functional magnetic resonance imaging (fMRI)   a medical imaging method that uses oxygen flow to measure activation in certain areas of the brain

going viral   the phenomenon of massive sharing of e-mails, blog postings, videos, and other content across social networks such that the content is viewed and shared by millions of people within minutes or hours

graphical user interface (GUI)   the portion of software that includes windows, menus, buttons, checkboxes, drop-down lists, and other visual components that can display information to the user and receive input from the user

graphical user interface (GUI) builder   software that allows programmers to design GUIs by drawing components of the GUIs on-screen rather than by writing textual instructions

Health Insurance Portability and Accountability Act (HIPAA)   a U.S. federal law passed in 1996 that standardizes and controls access to electronic medical records to both facilitate their use and to protect patient privacy

human cloud   the group of always available, skilled workers available for freelancing

ignorantia iuris non excusat a   Latin legal term meaning "ignorance of the law is no excuse"; it implies that a person's lack of knowledge that a particular act was unlawful does not absolve that person of legal liability for performing the act

industrial robots   robots developed to perform specific tasks; frequently used in tightly controlled environments, such as on assembly lines

industry   a set of businesses that provide similar services or offer similar products; oil, agriculture, and automobiles are examples of products that define separate industries

integrated circuit (IC) a miniaturized electronic circuit that has been manufactured in the surface of a thin substrate of semiconductor material; also known as a chip or microchip

integrated development environment (IDE) software used by programmers to provide unified control over a variety of programming tools, such as compilers, linkers, and debuggers

interrogatory a formal set of questions provided by one party in a lawsuit to the other party as part of DISCOVERY, for the purpose of establishing matters of fact and to determine which facts will be presented at trial

intranet a privately maintained computer network that is used to connect computers within an organization; an intranet is only available to members of the organization, not to the general public

Jacquard loom a loom that could automatically weave patterns into cloth by processing cards into which holes had been punched; an early example of a programmable machine

Java a computer programming language and platform that makes it possible to write a single set of source code for a computer program and to compile that source code to be executed on multiple platforms

Java runtime environment software designed specifically for a particular computer platform to enable Java bytecode to execute on it; different Java runtime environments exist for different computer platforms to enable all of them to execute the same Java bytecode without the need to recompile that bytecode separately for each platform

just-in-time distribution a supply chain model that takes orders and payments before products are made at the factory, to enable products to be manufactured only if and when they are ordered by customers

knowledge worker a worker who is paid to act and communicate with knowledge in a specific subject area rather than to manufacture physical products or perform other physical labor; examples of knowledge workers are financial analysts, computer programmers, news reporters, and marketing consultants

laparoscope the camera used during laparoscopic surgery

laparoscopic surgery   a minimally invasive surgical technique in which a small incision is made away from the site of surgery and a camera and surgical tools are inserted, moved into position, and controlled with a joystick

lawyer in a box   software, such as Quicken Family Lawyer, that can help individuals prepare wills, contracts, bills of sale, and other legal documents without hiring a human lawyer

linker   software that links together multiple object code files to create a larger program

machine language   the code language that is understood and directly executable by a computer's processor; object code is in the form of machine language

magnetic resonance imaging (MRI)   a medical imaging method capable of using powerful magnets to create a very high resolution picture of internal organs and bones

mail merge   a software function in which multiple documents, such as form letters, are produced from a single template and a data source

mass production   the production of large amounts of standardized products, usually in factories and on assembly lines

Mechanical Turk   Amazon's crowdsourcing platform that allows people to post projects to be completed by members of the community, called Turkers

medical decision support software   an interactive diagnostic tool for medical professionals that assists in making diagnoses, prescribing medicines, and recommending treatment of patients

neuroimaging   a variety of techniques used to take photographs or build models of the brain

object   a structure created by a program written in an object-oriented programming language to perform a particular function and to store particular data

object code   the machine-readable code that a computer processor executes; usually created by using a compiler to translate source code into object code

object-oriented programming language   a programming language, such as Smalltalk, C++, or Java, which enables programs to be written that define programs in terms of objects that communicate with each other

operations manuals documents, often printed on paper, that contain instructions to be followed by employees of a business to perform common business functions, such as sorting incoming mail, requesting vacation time, or reserving a conference room

outsourcing the contracting out of a business function, previously performed in-house by a company, to another company

paperless office an office in which all data are stored in electronic form, such as in word processing documents, spreadsheets, and databases, and in which all communication among people is performed using electronic means such as telephone, fax, e-mail, and instant messaging

parametering a customization approach that allows customers to select the features they want, then receive a product recommendation that addresses their needs

phonograph an instrument for reproducing sounds by means of the vibration of a stylus or needle following a spiral groove on a revolving disc or cylinder

photolithography a process used in the manufacture of semiconductor devices in which an image is transferred from a photograph onto a substrate, producing a pattern that acts as a mask during an engraving process

plaintiff the accusing party in a lawsuit

platform a combination of computer hardware and software that serves as the foundation for all hardware that connects to a computer and all software that runs on the computer; examples of computer platforms include the WinTel and Mac platforms

popularizing a mass customization approach in which a manufacturer offers customers a limited product line that is updated regularly

positron emission tomography (PET) medical imaging method that uses radioactively-tagged oxygen to track, over time, how much oxygen flow different areas of the brain receive

prescription errors any error that causes a patient to receive a prescription that is different than the doctor intended, such as a prescription for the wrong medication or the wrong dosage of the right medication; one of the leading preventable forms of hospital error

procedural programming language a programming language which enables programs to be written in the form of sequences of instructions that define procedures

process control activities involved in ensuring a process is predictable, stable, and consistently operating at target performance levels

profession a set of skills, ethical rules, and customs that define a particular trade; law, medicine, accounting, and teaching are examples of professions

programming language a language in which computer programmers write computer programs; examples include C, C++, C#, Java, and Pascal

punched cards paper cards into which holes have been punched to control a Jacquard loom or to provide instructions to early computers

quality assurance (QA) the systematic process of testing products such as machines and software before they are sold to ensure that they are free from flaws

res ipsa loquitur a Latin term used in the law to mean "the thing speaks for itself"; in tort law, it means that the facts themselves indicate that the defendant must be at fault, even if there is no direct evidence that the defendant performed an act that caused harm to the plaintiff

rich media advertisements online advertising that leverages technology such as Adobe Flash to display interactive advertisements containing audio and video

robot a mechanical device capable of performing physical tasks on command or through advance programming; may also be operated by remote control

robotics technology dealing with the design, construction, and operation of robots

scientific management the practice of using scientific research to determine the most efficient method of performing a task; incorporated the selection and training of workers who are to perform the task and the division of labor between managers and workers

search advertisements online advertisements placed on search engine result pages; search advertisements typically advertise products and services that relate to the displayed search results

search engine optimization (SEO) modifications make to a Web site by Web development professionals to increase the likelihood that the Web site will appear on the first page of the search results produced by search engines such as Google

shared hard drive a digital electronic storage device that can be accessed by multiple users so that files can be stored, modified, and read by those users without needing to store separate copies of the files on each user's personal hard drive

SharePoint a system for managing documents, e-mail messages, and other data among multiple users, developed by Microsoft Corporation

***Shepard's* Citations Service** a list of all authorities citing a particular case, statute, or legal authority; often used by lawyers to determine whether a court's ruling in one case was subsequently overturned by another ruling in a later case

shorthand a system of rapid note-taking in which only the stylized outlines of words and phrases are written; once commonly used in offices to record dictated letters and reports

social mobility the ability for someone who was born into one social class to move into a different social class during his or her lifetime; widespread social mobility is often considered a sign of a modern economy

software as a service (SaaS) a delivery model in which software and data are hosted on the Internet and accessed remotely using a client such as a Web browser, instead of being installed directly on the user's computer; user's typically pay a monthly subscription fee for SaaS products instead of making a one-time payment for lifetime use of the product

software quality assurance (SQA) the use of automated processes as a means of checking the functionality of software code and scanning for errors

source code the human-readable instructions that a computer programmer writes in a programming language to create software

stenography the process of writing in shorthand

stress testing the process of using a product until it fails, often under stresses such as increasing vibration, temperature, or humidity

supply chain the complete set and sequence of suppliers required to provide a particular product or service; the supply chain for a box of cereal might include the farm that grows the grain, the mill that processes the grain into flour, the cereal manufacturer that makes and packages the cereal, the distributer that transports the cereal to the supermarket, and the supermarket that sells the cereal to consumers

supply chain management the process of automating, optimizing, and implementing an efficient supply chain, typically using software and the Internet

switching costs the cost associated with switching from one task to another in contrast to performing the same task continuously; one goal of the division of labor is to minimize switching costs

tailoring a customization approach that invites the customer to provide product specifications (often from a limited menu of options) from the beginning of the manufacturing process

Taylorism a production method developed by Frederick Winslow Taylor that divides every work task into segments that can be easily analyzed and taught; the practice of scientific management

teleoperated robot (telerobot) a robot controlled from a distance by a human operator rather than following a programmed sequence of movements

template a document in which standardized portions are already completed and variable portions can be completed using a document management system

text editor a program for editing text, often used by computer programmers to write source code

time and motion studies timed observations of a worker's production process, with the goal of finding the most efficient way to perform a particular task; a feature of scientific management

transistor an electronic device used to control the flow of electricity in electronic equipment; forms the basis for modern integrated circuits used in computers

Turker someone who completes jobs posted on Amazon's Mechanical Turk crowdsourcing platform

Unimate a robotic arm first used for auto assembly by General Motors in 1962; the first universally accepted piece of robotic hardware in the workplace

variable text in document assembly software, the text (such as the name and address of the recipient of a letter) that varies from one copy of a document to another

varietizing a customization approach that offers customers a range of products in several varieties, such as five dress designs in 10 colors each

virtual accident reconstruction technology that allows experts to reconstruct the scene of an accident from pictures and measurements taken at a scene of an accident in order to produce a 3D rendering of the accident scene, often for use in court

virtual company a business that uses electronic means, rather than traditional brick-and-mortal office space, to conduct its operations

virtual office an office that is rented by a business by the hour to use as-needed instead of for a priced rent per month; companies that lease virtual offices often also provide their tenants with permanent phone numbers and mailing addresses to provide the appearance to their customers of having a fixed permanent office

word processing an electronic editing and publishing process invented by IBM in the late 1960s; originally referred to any machine that processed words, such as dictating machines and ordinary electric typewriters, but now most commonly implemented in word processing software

workflow automation software software that is programmed with knowledge of the steps involved in a performing a particular business process and the people who are responsible for performing each step, and which guides those people through all of the steps in the process to ensure that those steps are performed correctly, on time, and by the appropriate people

WYSIWYG (what you see is what you get)   a program that allows a user to see what the end result will look like while the interface or document is being created

X-ray computed tomography (CT) scans   a medical imaging method that is capable of generating a 3-D image of the inside of an object from a series of 2-D X-ray slices

zealous advocacy   the requirement that an attorney vigorously represent the interests of his or her clients in court, in negotiations with other parties, and in all other dealings in an attempt to obtain the best possible outcome for the client

FURTHER RESOURCES

The following resources are arranged according to chapter title.

"Scientific Management: The Systematization of Work"

BOOKS

Head, Simon. *The New Ruthless Economy: Work and Power in the Digital Age.* Oxford: Oxford University Press, 2003. The author points to information technology as the prime cause of growing wage disparity.

ARTICLES

Bautz, Greer. "The New Division of Labor: How Computers Are Creating the Next Job Market." Harvard Graduate School of Education, June 1, 2004. Available online. URL: www.gse.harvard.edu/news/features/murnane06012004.html. Accessed July 8, 2011. An interview with economists and authors Richard Murnane and Frank Levy.

Heiser, Herman. "The Application of Computers to Scientific Management." *Analysts Journal.* Available online. URL: http://www.jstor.org/pss/4529367. Accessed July 8, 2011. A 1958 review of the applications of computers to business systems.

Takeuchi, Hirotaka, Emi Osono, and Norihiko Shimizu. "The Contradictions That Drive Toyota's Success." *Harvard Business Review* (June 2008). A report on a six-year study of the Toyota Production System, which calls it necessary but insufficient to account for Toyota's success.

WEB SITES

BusinessDictionary.com. Available online. URL: www.businessdictionary.com. Accessed July 8, 2011. Definitions of business and economic terms.

NetMBA.com. Available online. URL: www.netmba.com. Accessed July 8, 2011. Definitions and explanations of business and economic terms.

"Manufacturing: From Line Workers to Robots"

ARTICLES

Babineau, Marc Phillipe. "A Look at How the Automobile Industry Uses Robots." Helium.com Web site. Available online. URL: www.helium.com/items/1404007-a-look-at-how-the-automobile-industry-uses-robots. Accessed July 8, 2011. Weighs in on the pros and cons of robot-controlled tasks in automotive manufacturing.

Cox, W. Michael. "Mass Customization." Federal Reserve Bank of Dallas Web site. Available online. URL: http://www.dallasfed.org/eyi/tech/9909custom.html. Accessed July 8, 2011. Asks and answers the question: Why have Americans had to wait until the tail end of the 20th century for mass customization?

Ganapati, Priya. "3-D Printers Make Manufacturing Accessible." Wired.com Web site. Available online. URL: www.wired.com/gadgetlab/2009/08/makerbot. Accessed July 8, 2011. An intriguing glimpse into the world of do-it-yourself 3-D printing.

Noagi, Elizabeth G. "Ready Wear Clothing: Mass Production and Mass Customization." University of Washington, March 17, 2010. Available online. URL: http://readywearclothing.wordpress.com. Accessed July 8, 2011. A research presentation on the development of mass clothing production and how digital technology is affecting the apparel industry.

Pethokoukis, James M. "Meet Your New Coworker: Industrial Robots Are Reshaping Manufacturing." *U.S. News and World Report.* Available online. URL: www.usnews.com/usnews/biztech/articles/040315/15eerobots.htm. Accessed July 8, 2011. A discussion of whether American workers are losing jobs to machines as companies look to increase productivity.

Plotkin, Robert. "Simulating Auto Assembly." Automating Invention blog post, May 17, 2009. Available online. URL: www.automatinginvention.com. Accessed July 8, 2011. A blog that deals with the impact of computer-automated inventing on the future of invention and patent law.

WEB SITES

Robotics Online. Available online. URL: www.robotics.org. Accessed March 10, 2011. This site is sponsored by the Robotic Industries Association, a trade group that serves the robotics industry.

"Administrative Assistants: From Typist to Office Manager"

ARTICLES

"Carbons to Computers: A Short History of the Birth and Growth of the American Office." Smithsonian Institution Web site. Available online. URL: http://www.smithsonianeducation.org/educators/lesson_plans/carbons/text/birth.html. Accessed July 8, 2011. Explores the changing American office, from the 1830s to the late twentieth century, as a way to study the nation's growth from the industrial revolution to the information age.

Davis, Cheryl. "Automatic Speech Recognition and Access." *Hearing Loss* (2001). Available online. URL: http://www.wou.edu/education/sped/wrocc/asr.htm. Accessed July 8, 2011. A discussion of how breakthroughs in technology have made automatic speech recognition a reality.

Juang, B. H., and Lawrence Rabiner. "Automatic Speech Recognition—A Brief History of the Technology." *Elsevier Encyclopedia of Language and Linguistics,* Second Edition. Available online. URL: www.ece.ucsb.edu/Faculty/Rabiner/ece259/Reprints/354_LALI-ASRHistory-final-10-8.pdf. Accessed July 8, 2011. A review of highlights in the research and development of automatic speech recognition during the past few decades.

Ng, Deb. "How the Internet Changed the Way We Work." Kommein.com blog post. Available online. URL: http://kommein.com/how-the-internet-changed-the-way-work. Accessed July 8, 2011. A personal reminiscence of working in an office before the advent of computers, e-mail, and iPhones.

Smith, William D. "Lag Persists for Business Equipment." *New York Times,* October 26, 1971. Excerpt available online. URL: http://tinyurl.com/4v75oky. Accessed July 8, 2011. An article from the dawn of the word processing age, dealing with the technology's potential impact on the work force.

"Managers: Business Information at Your Fingertips"

BOOKS

Levinson, William. *Henry Ford's Lean Vision: Enduring Principles from the First Ford Motor Plant.* New York: Productivity Press, 2002. Taken from Ford's own journals, Lean Vision is a description of what made Ford successful and a discussion of how business can maintain these enduring principles.

ARTICLES

Aksoy, Yasemin. "Supply Chain Management." *Or/MS Today.* Available online. URL: http://www.lionhrtpub.com/orms/orms-6-03/scm.html. Accessed July 8, 2011. Research indicates that supply chain management remains a top priority for industry executives interested in optimizing processes.

Bender, Eric. "Three Minutes: Godfathers of the Spreadsheet." *PC World* Web site. Available online. URL: http://www.pcworld.com/article/116166/three_minutes_godfathers_of_the_spreadsheet.html. Accessed July 8, 2011. A description of the creation of VisiCalc and how, within three years, it became an application that every accountant needed.

"IBM's Brill Says Email Is Overrated." IT Jungle Web site. Available online. URL: http://www.itjungle.com/tfh/tfh040411-story05.html. Accessed July 8, 2011. A look at why e-mail is best used as an alerting system instead of a collaborative discussion medium.

Kissell, Joe. "How to Make Your Office Paperless." *ComputerWorld* Web site. Available online. URL: http://news.idg.no/cw/art.cfm?id=7BD8E700-1A64-6A71-CE01A12CD96D26E4. Accessed July 8, 2011. A modern attempt at building a paperless office, including instructions for scanning paper documents using OCR to create searchable documents.

Lynn, Samara. "Intuit Takes Cue from Apple, Shows Off App Store, New Tech." *PC Magazine* Web site. Available online.URL: http://www.pcmag.com/article2/0,2817,2382837,00.asp. Accessed July 8, 2011. Intuit launches an integrated app center for all of its products in a cloud-based, software as a service (SaaS) model.

"The Office of the Future." *BusinessWeek.* Available online. URL: http://www.businessweek.com/technology/content/may2008/tc20080526_547942.htm. Accessed April 5, 2010. An article in a 1975 issue of *BusinessWeek* describing one writer's conception of a paperless office.

WEB SITES

SalesForce.com. Available online. URL: http://www.salesforce.com. Accessed July 8, 2011. Industry leader in CRM software.

"Computer Programmers: Creating Software for Creating Software"

BOOKS

Dijkstra, Edsger W. *Selected Writings on Computing: A Personal Perspective.* Berlin: Springer-Verlag, 1982. A collection of writings from one of computer science's most influential pioneers.

Grier, David Alan. *When Computers Were Human.* Princeton: Princeton University Press, 2005. A historical account of the people who worked as human "computers" to perform calculations by hand before automated computers were invented.

McConnell, Steve. *Code Complete: A Practical Handbook of Software Construction.* Redmond, Wash.: Microsoft Press, 1993. A comprehensive guide to designing, writing, and testing computer programs, written for both novice and expert programmers and managers.

ARTICLES

Bergin, Joseph, and Russel Winder. "Understanding Object-Oriented Programming." Available online. URL: http://csis.pace.edu/~bergin/patterns/ppoop.html. Accessed July 8, 2011. An introduction to object-oriented programming, targeted at readers who have at least some experience with non-object-oriented programming.

Fei, Zongming. "GUI Builder Tools." Available online. URL: http://www.cc.gatech.edu/classes/cs6751_97_winter/Topics/gui-builder. Accessed July 8, 2011. An overview and discussion of the advantages and disadvantages of graphical user interface builders.

O'Dell, Jolie. "A Beginner's Guide to Integrated Development Environments." Available online. URL: http://mashable.com/2010/10/06/ide-guide. Accessed July 8, 2011. In introduction to and overview of various integrated development environments for use by computer programmers.

Sureau, Denis. "History of Programming Languages and Their Evolution." Available online. URL: http://www.scriptol.com/programming/history.php. Accessed July 8, 2011. Provides a chronological listing and description of a large number of programming languages throughout the history of computing.

WEB SITES

Admiral Grace Murray Hopper. Available online. URL: http://www.sdsc. edu/ScienceWomen/hopper.html. Accessed July 8, 2011. A short biography of influential computer scientist Grace Hopper, who designed the first software compiler.

Computer Languages History. Available online. URL: http://www.levenez. com/lang. Accessed July 8, 2011. Provides a graphical timeline illustrating the history of computer programming languages.

Edsger W. Dijkstra Archive. Available online. URL: http://www.cs.utexas. edu/users/EWD. Accessed July 8, 2011. The collected manuscripts of computer scientist Edsger W. Dijkstra.

Java. Available online. URL: http://www.java.com. Accessed July 8, 2011. The official Web site of the Java platform.

Object-Oriented Programming Tutorial. Available online. URL: http:// www.aonaware.com/OOP1.htm. Accessed July 8, 2011. A step-by-step introduction to the key concepts of object-oriented programming.

"Law: From Parchment to PCs"

ARTICLES

Garvin, Peggy. "The Government Domain: GovTrack and OpenCongress Go Beyond THOMAS." LLRX Web site. Available online. URL: http://www. llrx.com/columns/govdomain25.htm. Accessed July 8, 2011. New services aggregate the freely available congressional records and provide new features for following legislative procedure.

Jacoby, Conrad J. "E-Discovery Update: Pushing Back Against Hardcopy ESI Productions." LLRX Web site. Available online. URL: http://www.llrx. com/columns/hardcopyesi.htm. Accessed July 8, 2011. Information about metadata stored in electronically-discovered documents and why converting them to paper can be harmful to a case.

Strutin, Ken. "Forensic Evidence and the CSI Effect." LLRX Web site. Available online. URL: http://www.llrx.com/features/forensicevidencecsieffect. htm. Accessed July 8, 2011. A description of how juries across America are influenced by the cut-and-dried forensic work on Hollywood crime dramas.

WEB SITES

Duke University Web site. Available online. URL: http://www.law.duke.edu/lib/researchguides/intresearch. Accessed July 8, 2011. A resource of free legal research sites, government information, legislation, court decisions, and more.

Findlaw Web site. Available online. URL: http://www.findlaw.com. Accessed July 8, 2011. Westlaw's free legal research search engine.

Legal Research Tutorial. Available online. URL: http://www.west.net/~smith/lrmain-content.htm. Accessed July 8, 2011. An online tutorial for performing legal research.

LexisNexis Web site. Available online. URL: http://www.lexisnexis.com. Accessed July 8, 2011. Legal research search engine.

Richard Susskind's Web site. Available online. URL: http://www.susskind.com. Accessed July 8, 2011. Richard Susskind specializes in the use of technology in the legal field and in prognosticating on the future impact of technology on law.

United States Courts Web site. Available online. URL: http://www.uscourts.gov/CourtRecords.aspx. Accessed July 8, 2011. PACER provides electronic access to court records.

Westlaw Web site. Available online. URL: http://www.westlaw.com. Accessed July 8, 2011. Legal research search engine.

"Medicine: Doctors Enter the Digital Age"

ARTICLES

Burton, Robert. "Long-distance Surgery." Salon Web site. Available online. URL: http://www.salon.com/health/col/bob/2000/01/31/telemedicine. Accessed July 8, 2011. Telemedicine allows doctors to operate remotely in war zones.

Dawson, D. L., J. Lee Meyer, and E. S. Pevec, WC. "Training with Simulation Improves Residents' Endovascular Procedure Skills." *Journal of Vascular Surgery* 45, no. 1 (January 2007): 149–154. Available online. URL: http://www.ncbi.nlm.nih.gov/pubmed/17210400. Accessed July 8, 2011. Research indicating that surgery simulation realistically improves key performance metrics.

"Hospital Medication Error Lawsuit Results in $5 Million Verdict." Available online. URL: http://www.aboutlawsuits.com/hospital-medication-error-lawsuit-verdict-5-million-2717. Accessed July 8, 2011. A Pennsylvania woman is awarded a $5 million settlement when a prescription error results in permanent brain damage.

"Long-distance Surgery: Patient in Rome, Doctors in California." Available online. URL: http://www.shortnews.com/start.cfm?id=7006. Accessed July 8, 2011. Doctors in California successfully performed 17 long distance operations on patients in Rome.

Moehr, Jochen. "To Morris F. Collen: Happy Ninetieth!" *Journal of the American Medical Informatics Association* 10, no. 6 (November 2003): 613–615. Available online. URL: http://www.ncbi.nlm.nih.gov/pmc/articles/PMC264442/. Accessed July 8, 2011. A biography of Morris Collen, pioneer in medical informatics.

Power, Dan. "A Brief History of Decision Support Systems." DSS Resources Web site. Available online. URL: http://dssresources.com/history/dsshistory.html. Accessed July 8, 2011. A historical look at how decision support systems developed and are used as expert systems.

"Privacy of Medical Records." Privacy Rights Clearinghouse Web site. Available online. URL: http://www.privacyrights.org/fs/fs8-med.htm. Accessed July 8, 2011. Facts about medical records privacy from a leading privacy advocate.

"Simulation-based Brain Surgery in Halifax Yields Breakthrough In Surgical Training and Rehearsal." National Research Council Canada Web site. Available online. URL: http://www.nrc-cnrc.gc.ca/eng/news/nrc/2009/08/26/virtual-surgery.html. Accessed July 8, 2011. The first neurosurgical simulation developed and tested.

WEB SITES

Matrix Pharma Web site. Available online. URL: http://www.matrixpharma.ca. Accessed July 8, 2011. Industry leaders in computer-assisted drug development.

Nuance Web site. Available online. URL: http://www.nuance.com/for-healthcare/by-solutions/speech-recognition/dragon-medical/index.htm. Accessed July 8, 2011. Dragon Medical is the industry's leading speech-to-text medical transcription application.

OpenClinical Web site. Available online. URL: http://www.openclinical.org/emr.html. Accessed July 8, 2011. An overview of the different types of electronic medical records.

Sweet, Larry. Neuropsychology Central Web site. Available online. URL: http://www.neuropsychologycentral.com/interface/content/links/page_ material/imaging/imaging _links.html. Accessed July 8, 2011. Neuroimaging tutorials, links, and literature.

U.S. Department of Health and Human Services. Available online. URL: http://www.hhs.gov/ocr/privacy. Accessed July 8, 2011. The Health Insurance Portability and Accountability Act of 1996 (HIPAA) portal.

"How Computers Are Changing the Nature of Work"

ARTICLES

"Editor Outsources Everyday Life to India" ABC News Web site. Available online. URL: http://abcnews.go.com/GMA/story?id=996544&page=1. Accessed July 8, 2011. The story of an Esquire editor who outsourced his life to Your Man in India.

Mieszkowski, Katherine. "I Make $1.45 a Week and I Love It." Salon Web site. Available online. URL: http://www.salon.com/technology/feature/2006/07/24/turks. Accessed July 8, 2011. Illustrates the sort of low-pay, low-skill work available at Amazon's Mechanical Turk.

"The Future of Outsourcing." *Business Week*. Available online. URL: http://www.businessweek.com/magazine/content/06_05/b3969401.htm. Accessed July 8, 2011. A report detailing the ways in which outsourcing is transforming the way businesses operate.

"What Is Outsourcing?" *Sourcing Mag* Web site. Available online. URL: http://www.sourcingmag.com/content/what_is_outsourcing.asp. Accessed July 8, 2011. A description of outsourcing and businesses that commonly outsource.

WEB SITES

Elance Web site. Available online. URL: http://www.elance.com. Accessed July 8, 2011. One of the most comprehensive e-lancing and outsourcing Web sites.

Mechanical Turk Web site. Available online. URL: https://www.mturk.com/mturk/welcome. Accessed July 8, 2011. Provider of crowdsourcing services.

Regus Web site. Available online. URL: http://www.regus.com. Accessed July 8, 2011. Provider of virtual office space.

Your Man in India. Available online. URL: http://www.yourmaninindia.com. Accessed July 8, 2011. An outsourcing Web site where users can hire an Indian person to perform day-to-day tasks including paying bills, writing letters, or making phone calls.

INDEX

Italic page numbers indicate illustrations.